Virtuous Woman versus Foolish Woman

A Constant Battle Within

Tracy Mitchell

Virtuous Woman versus Foolish Woman

A Constant Battle Within

Tracy Mitchell

Virtuous Woman versus Foolish Woman

Copyright © 2015 by Tracy Mitchell

All rights reserved. This book or any portion thereof may not be reproduced or used in any manner whatsoever without the express written permission of the author except for the use of brief quotations in a book review.

ISBN-13: 978-0-9864385-4-7
ISBN-10: 0986438545

TYRO Publishing Services http://www.tyropublishing.com
Ordering Information: For details, contact the author via email @ (blesswoman40@gmail.com)

Printed in the United States of America

Dedication

I dedicate this book to first my Heavenly Father who has blessed me with the wisdom and strength to birth this book.

To my husband Pastor Larry Mitchell and my 3 children Edric, Larry and Asya who has supported me from the beginning.

To my parents Annie and Leroy Davis who have encouraged me throughout my youth, to always put God first and to follow after my dreams and never give up until I accomplish them.

To my sister Santesha Johnson who put up with my complaining during birthing this birth, who also encourage me in so many ways.

To my brother Pastor Johnny Davis who spiritually birth me and raised me up in the Lord. And my brothers Gary Davis and Daniel Montgomery my role models because of your accomplishment it gave me hope to keep going.

I thank God for blessing me with such caring, supportive and amazing family.

To my spiritual mentors who encourage me to keep pushing and never give up: You ladies are greatly appreciated I could have never made it through my most difficult times if was not for your support.

My Publisher Robin Holloway: CEO & Founder of Tyro Publishing Services. Pastor Lashanda Jones, Minister Truley Finley, Author: Joy Jallah, Author: Tiffany Gills Domenia.

About This Book

Virtuous Woman versus Foolish Woman, is for women of God who are ready for change. Change in their character, mindset, marriage and their personal relationship with the God Almighty.

This book talks about the war that's going on within every born-again believer's mind and how we should take each thought seriously.

In this book you will learn the characteristics of a *virtuous* or *wise woman* and see why God's chosen women today should desire to become this woman.

This book will also introduce you to a characteristic of a *foolish woman* who we are all familiar with: a woman from our past who refuses to let us go until we are defeated!

In this book you will learn how to cast down strongholds and rebellious spirits that war against our minds daily. How to depend totally on the help of the Holy Spirit and allow God to shape and mold us into the image of His idea woman.

This warfare that every woman has to endure are assigned by satan to prevent us from receiving our spiritual inheritance and from living out our God given purpose.

After reading this book, I pray that your life will never be the same and you will know, without a doubt, the battle is not ours its the Lord!

My Testimony, which lead to birthing this book.

When God first gave me this message four years ago, I ask, "Lord, what if I can give you some of my old self?" I had a desire to become a *virtuous woman* but didn't quite have the revelation of her. Immediately I heard the Spirit of the Lord say, "*A Spiritual death must take place first; this woman cannot be contaminated.*" Right then I had a revelation about Proverbs 31:10; now I understand what the bible says about *who can find this virtuous woman* because not many of us are willing to die to become her.

While I preached this message, I thought I had my life in order. My heart was fixed on God and I was heading in the right direction. My heart was determined to become this new woman and no devil in hell was going to stop me. I meditated on this woman for years. One of my favorite scriptures was *Proverbs 31*. I read books, and magazines; I went to workshops and conferences I even preached my own sermon about the virtuous woman. I had all of the head knowledge but no revelation.

During my prayer time, I would seek the Lord, asking Him what had I done wrong and why I couldn't see her in me when I looked into the mirror. In my mind I was doing everything right; I was submissive to my husband, and my house and kids were in order. *What's going on Lord?* I'm ready to experience how it feels to walk with the *virtuous woman* mindset. I had no clue that I would have to fight another spirit that kept me from totally surrendering to this virtuous woman who walks after the Heart of God.

One day I realized that God answered my prayer and told me to write this book; then Hell woke up and the battle began.

After totally surrendering my life and body to God, the battle between my flesh and spirit or (foolish woman and virtuous) began. See my old self was not going to bow down and die over night.

For the first time as a Christian, I was standing right in the midst of spiritual war that I wasn't prepared spiritually to encounter. I thought that by being a good Christian and not going and looking for sin, I wasn't making any room for the devil and was not in harm's way, but I was terribly wrong.

I've always had a fire for God. The thought of walking away or giving up was not on my to-do list, until I felt that I didn't have the strength to endure temptation anymore. How I used to try to escape was now no longer an option.

There I was, yielding to the flesh like never before, sometimes forgetting that I'm a woman of God. My prayer is, *Lord, shape and mold me into a virtuous woman. Change me Oh God! I don't know if I can take this.*"

If it wasn't for the word that was sown in my heart, I wouldn't have made it. I just knew that I was going to backslide and walk away from my First Love. My old self wanted my soul, body and mind. *She came to fight.* She knew me well and knew exactly what I liked. I lived in her body (old mindset) most of my life, but what she didn't realize was that I wasn't giving up without a fight, I had too much to live for now.

God had impregnated me with destiny and purpose, and I wasn't giving up my spiritual baby. *Somebody had to lose, and wasn't going to be me.*

Content

Dedication		*5*
About This Book		*7*
Acknowledgments		*12*

Chapter 1	Foolish Woman Versus Virtuous Woman: A Constant Battle Within!	15
Chapter 2	The Characteristics of the Foolish Woman	26
Chapter 3	Warring Against One Another!	34
Chapter 4	God's Plans for a Wife is the Same Yesterday, Today and Forever	39
Chapter 5	A Virtuous Woman Knows How to Speak and Seek Wisdom	49
Chapter 6	A Foolish Mindset Versus a Submissive Mindset	57
Chapter 7	Spiritual Desires versus Fleshly Desires A Constant Battle Within	66
Chapter 8	A Virtuous Woman Must Be Delivered from Ungodly Desires	80
Chapter 9	Taking Authority Over Strongholds That Our Old Mindset Created!	91

Chapter 10	A Foolish Mindset with Strongholds Leads to a Spirit of Rebellion	101
Chapter 11	God is the Potter and We are the Clay	109
Chapter 12	Transformation from Past Hurts	122

About the Author 136

Acknowledgments

Read what others are saying about Author Tracy Mitchell!

Your post inspire me! You are such a true woman of God and I can feel the power of your words! I love reading your post as they push me to live real and just be amazing

Master Coach/ Author Tish Bell

I met Tracy a few months ago on Facebook , she was giving spiritual advice to another person on FB as I read her post I was touched. Although I had never physically met her or spoken with her . I felt compelled to reach out to her in her inbox on FB. She responded to me as I asked if I could reach out to her by phone and she agreed. The first time we spoke I knew in my heart we would be sisters for life. She comforted me right away with her words of encouragement. I knew she understood me in more ways than I could explain. For she was a blessing at the right time when I wanted to just say forget it! Since then she has really inspired and encouraged me to step out in my own ministry and not be afraid. Just do it anyway. I will always love this lady. Love you for life!

Pastor Cassandra

Co-Pastor Tracy has encouraged me in so many ways. She trusted the God in me and allow me to assist her with her Woman to Woman Let's Talk About It conference calls someone who she hardly knew. She allow the Holy Spirit to use me freely. There were time I reached out to her and she never judged me, she just listen and said I understand. She saw the calling on my life when no one else could see it. I'm grateful for her word of love and correction that's needed in my life to help push me into my calling.

Robin Washington

Co-Pastor Tracy Mitchell inspired me, she's such a powerful woman of god, her mere presence inspire others as well, but for me her encouraging words, thoughtfulness and daily messages inspires me the most, its almost like she are speaking directly to me, and how she prayed with me the night I gave my life over to God. The powerful message she gave at my son's celebration and home going encouraged me during my most difficult times, any woman who allow God to use her to reach His people in a positive way, inspires me, she have no idea of the love I have for her. I look on fb every morning to see what message she have for us who having a hard time coping with things. She motivate me to keep pushing forward and let God continue to guide my path and I am ever so grateful. Her conference calls inspire me as well because when I think I am alone, there are other women who struggle just like me, I have to think ,I am really not alone, and when I think my life is bad, someone else is having an even harder time than me, so I feel truly blessed and with her as my Spiritual Mentor, there's nothing my God couldn't do but continue to order my steps in his Holy word. I give God praise for the gift that's in her.

Tameka Williams

Chapter 1

Foolish Woman Versus Virtuous Woman: A Constant Battle Within!

There's a warfare taking place within the mindset of every believer, male and female. This book will not only set you free in your mind but will also help free the minds of those you come in contact with on a daily basis.

In this chapter, I would like to introduce to you a woman whom we as Women of God have discussed in conferences, within our homes, and in our church communities. It is the Characteristic of God's Ideal Woman!

A foolish woman and virtuous woman each represent a Kingdom: A Kingdom of Darkness and a Kingdom of God. Lets start off by reading what the word of God has to say about a virtuous woman. A Virtuous woman is capable, intelligent, pure, holy, and walks in an excellent, submissive spirit. Every true woman of God should desire to become her. She's

God's ideal woman created for God. She is the apple of His eyes. *Proverbs 31:10-11, "Who can find a virtuous woman? For her price is far above rubies. The heart of her husband doth safely trust in her, so that he shall have no need of spoil.*

Proverbs 19:14 "House and riches are the inheritance from parents, but a wise, understanding, and prudent (Intelligent) wife is from the Lord."

Proverb 12:4 says, A virtuous and worthy wife (earnest and strong in character) is a crowning joy to her husband, but she who makes him a shame is as rottenness in his bones.

You may be reading these scriptures and shouting, *Lord help me!!* Believe me when I say that I understand. When God first gave me this message to preach five years ago, I felt the same way. I even tried to make a deal with Him by asking, *What if I give you some of my old self.*

I immediately heard the Spirit of the Lord say, *I need all of you. Half just won't do.*

My heart was determined to become this new woman and no devil in hell was going to stop me. My life where heading in the right direction: household in order, submissive to my husband. Life couldn't be any better than this. Then all of a sudden, like a head on collision, I faced this familiar spirit, my old self, that sinful, *Foolish Woman* I'd thought I had left behind the day I accepted Christ.

She refused to die: she had a goal to bring me down!

This woman wanted my body, soul and mind. I will talk more about her character in the following chapter, but first lets look at the character of the *virtuous woman*. This will explain why Satan puts up a fight to win me and everyone who desires to please God.

Matthew 22:37 says, "Thou shalt love the Lord thy God with all thy heart, and with all thou soul and with all thy Mind."

A *Virtuous Woman* serves God with all of her heart, mind, and soul. She seeks His will for her life, and she gives Him all of her, not just some of her time. She is a woman of Faith.

Prov 31:11 says, "The heart of her husband doth safely trust in her, so that he shall have no need of spoil."

Let's take a second to analyze Proverbs 31:11-12

A *virtuous woman* respects her husband. She does him good all the days of her life. She is trustworthy and a helpmate. If she brings anything that does not line up to God's word, she is out of order.

You may say, "Well, no marriage is perfect: we all makes mistakes." I would say that you are absolutely correct, but that truth doesn't change God's word concerning how a wife should submit. With the help of the Holy Spirit and balance along with wisdom, we can be transformed into this mighty woman of God.

I will go into further details in Chapter 4 concerning God's idea wife for His *men of valor*. Until then, lets turn our focus back on the character of a virtuous woman.

A *Virtuous Woman* does not complains while completing her tasks: She's a hard working woman who has a serving spirit. She loves serving her husband, family, friends and neighbors with a gentle and loving spirit.

Proverbs 31:13 says, "She seeketh wool and flax and works with willing hands (to develop) it."

When we complain about the task that God has given us as a wife and mother including our vocation, we walk in a *foolish woman* mindset, not showing Him gratitude for what He has blessed us with each day.

In addition to showing God gratitude, take time out everyday to show gratitude to your husband. Let him know how much you appreciate being his wife. Yes, it will take some submissiveness on your part, but it can be done.

A *Virtuous Woman* uses her time wisely: A virtuous woman is busy working for the Lord and taking care of her family daily. She never has time for drama or to dwell on things that are not pleasing to God or her husband. There is nothing perfect about this woman of God: she just walks in a mature mindset.

Proverbs 31:14 says, "She is like a merchant's ships: she bringeth her food from afar." What ever needs to be done, this woman of God will make it happen.

Sometimes drama will come into our lives, but that doesn't mean we have to dwell on it. Change your environment or circle if needed: do whatever it takes to walk in this wise woman's mindset. God gave us time for the purpose to serve Him and His people, and we need to use this time wisely.

Philippians 4:8 says, "Finally brethen, whatsoever things are true whatsoever things are honest, whatsoever things are just, whatsoever things are pure, whatsoever things are of good report, if there be any Virtue, and if there be any praise think on these things (set your minds on them)."

A *Virtuous Woman* always has a word in her mouth: A virtuous woman loves and enjoys ministering, not only to her family and church family, but others as well. Everybody who comes around her admires and adores her caring and loving spirit. It brings me joy when I hear someone tell me that they love my spirit and caring heart. It lets me know that I'm pleasing God and letting His light shine. We all have days when we don't want to be entertained or bothered, but that shouldn't prevent us from walking in love.

Proverbs 31:15 says, "She riseth also while it is yet night, and giveth meat to her household and portion to her maidens." She gives spiritually and naturally to all of those whom she comes in contact with.

A Virtuous Woman Handles her Finances and Knows How To Budget:

Proverbs 31:16 says, "She considereth a field, and buyeth it with the fruit of her hands, she planteth a vineyard."

I believe it's safe to say that most of us, as women, have or still do struggle in this area. We love to spend money. It's our nature to do so, but a virtuous or wise woman seeks her husband's approval before making a purchase. She spends money wisely, not like it grows on a tree. She is a woman who knows how to budget. I never spend a dime without asking my husband if it would be okay, even though I earn my own paycheck. I believe in unity. God said that we are one and that includes our money.

You may be reading this and saying to yourself, *"Well, Tracy, how can we budget money we don't have?"* Easy, don't spend money you can't afford to spend.

When finances are difficult in a household, this makes place for the enemy to come in and bring stress, strife and bitterness between a husband and wife. If you have the spirit of greed, you need to ask the Holy Spirit to help you, because it will rob you from your faith and in trusting God. Remember money is a seed not your source.

1 Timothy 6:10 says,"For love of money is the root of all evil which while some coveted after, they have erred from the faith, and pierced themselves through with many sorrows."

Proverbs 31:17 says, "She girdeth her loins with strength, and strengtheneth her arms." AMP version says, "*She girds herself with strength (spiritual, mental, and physical fitness for her God-given task) and makes her arms strong and firm.*

A Virtuous Woman takes care of her physical body: A wise woman should prepare healthy food for her family, but most of us do not, We understand that being healthy and not sick all the time will benefit us in the Kingdom of God. How can we do the work of the Lord if we are sick with high blood pressure and diabetes? It's possible: Christians do it everyday, but it's not God's will for us to be sick in our bodies.

Proverbs 31:17 says that a virtuous or wise woman girdeth her loins with strength, and strengtheneth her arms.

I love how the AMP version states that she girds herself with strength (Mental, and Physical fitness for her God-given task) and make her arms strong and firm. It can't get any plainer than this. God holds us accountable for how we treat our bodies.

1 Corinthians 6:19: "Know ye not that your body is the temple of the Holy Ghost which is in you, which you have of God, and ye are not your own."

Proverbs 31:18- AMP says, "She tastes and sees that her gain from work(with and for God) is good; her lamp goeth not out, but it burns on continually through the night (of trouble, privation, or sorrow, warning away fear, doubt and distrust)."

A *Virtuous Woman* will forever let her light shine before and away from Men. She intercedes during all trials and tribulation for her husband and Children's needs. She walks with no fear when comes to taking care of her household.

A *Virtuous Woman* teaches her children the ways of her Father. She raise them up in the Lord and the Love of Christ. She believes the word of God.

Proverbs 22:6 AMP "Train up a child in the way he should go (and in keeping with his individual gift or bent), and when he is old he will not depart from it."

I am a living witness to this scripture. I have three beautiful children: Edric {26} Asya {20}, and Larry {22}. My husband Larry and I raised our children up in the Lord with the guidance of the Holy Spirit. They all serve the Lord today with all their hearts, souls and minds.

Raising your children up in the Lord is a lifestyle. Taking them to church every Sunday is a start, but living a Godly lifestyle around them when you are not in church will impact their lives in a more prosperous way.

Children need to see their parents living Holy life. Parents don't have to be perfect, but children should wake up everyday a Godly atmosphere. My children watch me closely. They didn't hesitate letting me know that I'm slipping or not walking in the will of God.

My children are well disciplined and never gave my husband and I any trouble. Yes, they tasted this world like most children of this world have done. They went astray but never departed from what they where raised to believe.

Today, my oldest son, Edric, is a gospel artist living out his God given purpose and is married to an beautiful woman of God, my daughter in law, Shatima. My son, Larry, just graduated from college and is a young man after God's own heart. He will soon follow after his dreams as a future actor. My beautiful daughter, Asya, is a virtuous young lady who attends college, as well. Her goal is to become a Dental Assistant. Praise God!! If you do what the word says, to raise your children up in the Lord, the same will happen for your family. God's word can't lie. We serve a God who shows no favoritism.

Last but not least, a *Virtuous Woman* is a woman of worth and beauty. She has an inner beauty that only comes from Christ.

If your response after reading this chapter is, "Tracy, I don't know if I can become this Virtuous Woman of God. I'm barely holding on to my salvation. Every time I come close to doing what's right, my flesh gets weak. My character does not always line up with the will of God. To be honest, most of the time I find myself yielding more to the flesh."

Don't condemn yourself! The day you totally surrender to God and give your life to Christ, you become by faith a Virtuous Woman of God. This Christian life we're living is by faith and grace. Who are we to boast?

As I explain the characteristic of a foolish woman in this next chapter I pray you will judge yourselves daily discipline your flesh until it lines up with the word of God.

Satan started this war or conflicts between God and the believers in Heaven he has always been an accuser of the brethren. Listen to the conversation that took place then you will understand that this war between satan and God is real.

Revelation 12:7-12 says and war broke out in heaven: Michael and his angels fought with dragon; and the dragon and his angels fought, but they did not prevail, nor was a place found for them in heaven any longer. So the great dragon was cast out, that serpent of old, called the devil satan, who deceives the whole world; he was cast to the earth, and his angels were cast out with him. Then I heard a loud voice saying in heaven, "Now salvation and strength, and the kingdom of our God, and the power of His Christ have come, for the accuser of our brethren, who accused them before our God day and night, has been cast down. And they overcame him by the blood of the Lamb and by the word of their testimony, and they did not love their lives to the death. Therefore rejoice, O heavens and you who dwell in them! Woe to the inhabitants of the earth and the sea! For the devil has come down to you, having great wrath, because he knows that he has a short time."

Now we see the conflicts and how things got started lets take a look at how the war begun. Satan knew he didn't have much time left and that his days were numbered so he went for blood and that's God's Kingdom!

Isaiah 14:12-15 How you have fallen from heaven, morning star, son of dawn! You have been cast down to the earth, you who once laid low nation's! You said in your heart, I will ascend to heavens; I will sit enthroned the mount of assembly, on the utmost heights of Mount Zaphon. I will ascend above the tops of the clouds; I will make myself like the Most High. But you are brought down to the realm of the dead, to the depths of the pit.

Now what I am about to say is not written in the bible, but I trust the Holy Spirit in me; I truly believe that when satan hit the ground, the war to get back with God began with His son and daughter Adam and Eve in the garden. *This warfare continues today.*

Chapter 2

The Characteristics of the Foolish Woman

Now that I've discuss and shared biblical scriptures concerning the Virtuous Woman, I would like to impart some wisdom and revelation concerning this war that's warring against our flesh. As you read this chapter, I pray your understanding would be enlightened and that you would compare both women and choose which one you would like to live. In my introduction, I spoke about this Foolish Woman who refuses to give up, she won't quit until she sees us defeated.

This woman or spirit is our old mindset, before we accepted our Lord and Savior. If you look at the word foolishness in the Webster's Dictionary it states that foolishness is the lack or failure of wisdom and of making proper careful choices. In this sense, it differs from stupidity, which is the lack of intelligence. An act of foolishness is called folly. Let's take a look at this word, folly is a lack of good sense, a person who is unwise and silly.

Proverb 9:13 says a foolish woman is noisy, she is simple and knoweth nothing. AMP version: says a foolish woman is noisy, she is simple and open to all forms of evil, she willfully and recklessly knows nothing whatever of eternal value. We all can relate to this woman. I recall before surrendering my life to Christ I loved the center of attention. I was open to all forms of evil. Whatever I wanted to do, to please my flesh I did it, no questions asked. I'm a grown woman and was not willing to listen to spiritual instruction. I knew everything!

Sad to say, this familiar spirit still wars against my flesh today. When I don't have my way, this familiar spirit raises her head and I constantly have to put her back in her rightful place. If you can relate, you are reading the right book. When we look at the character of this foolish woman, it may seem we are talking about an unbeliever. What I'm about to share with you, will change the way you think and see yourself. This Foolish Woman or old man lives within a *disobedient* Christian.

Time to Expose That Foolish Old Mindset and Be Set Free.

Lets start off by seeing what the Word of God has to say concerning a foolish or silly woman. 2 Timothy 3:6-7 says, *for of this sort are they which creep into houses, and lead captive silly women laden with sins, led away with divers lust.* AMP version: verse seven says, *these weak women will listen to anybody who will teach them. They are forever inquiring and getting information, but are never able to arrive at a recognition and knowledge of the Truth.*

We are facing a battle in the Body of Christ today as well, nothing new under the sun. Sad to say that sometimes we can find ourselves acting just like the women in *2 Timothy*. We must know that the battle is not flesh and blood, it's within our minds. I can imagine the excuses the women of God tried to explain after been exposed to this foolish mindset. I'm sure they blame the men of God, we need to daily give God praise for revelation and knowledge of His word.

Proverbs 12:15 says, *"The way of a fool is right in his own eyes, but he who listens to counsel is wise.* The bible says if we as believers seek not after Godly counsel but trust in our own understanding we acting like fools with no understanding. (Proverbs 3:5).

When we find ourselves yielding and obeying our old man (flesh) and immediately start making excuses for our disobedience, such as "I'm being myself" "I feel like I'm doing the right thing" "Nothing wrong with what I'm doing" " I can't help myself" and so on. It is evidence that your battle has begun.

Our spirit man (Virtuous Woman) if born again will bring back remembrance of what the Word of God says concerning that ungodly thought or unresolved issues that we battle within our minds with the *help* of The Holy Ghost. John 14:26 making no excuse for our disobedience John 14:26.

Proverbs 12:16 says, *A fool's wrath is presently known: but a prudent man covereth shame.* AMP version: *says a fool's wrath is quickly and openly known, but a prudent man ignores an insult.* The definition of *prudent* means *having good sense in dealing with practical matters.*

Every time we handle practical matters in an ungodly way by lashing out at our husband, children and our brothers and sisters who we come into contact with on a daily basis we're acting foolish. We all have our days when we act out on our emotions, no matter who is listening or watching. Time to put this foolish mindset back in its rightful place and that's in our past. Just because someone comes against us and we choose to to walk in integrity and follow after our virtuous spirit, doesn't make us a fool, it makes us wise and prudent.

The bible tells us to be a fool for Christ's sake not for our sake.1 Corinthians 4:10 AMP version says, *we are (looked upon as) fools on account of Christ and for His sake, but you (supposedly) are so amazingly wise and prudent in Christ! We are weak, but you (so very) strong! You highly esteemed, but we are in disrepute and contempt!*

Glory to God!! Tell your old man (Foolish Woman) from this day forth I choose with the help of the Holy Ghost my helper and a willing heart, to walk after this wise, prudent, with good character and integrity, virtuous woman that's living on the inside of me. I will not yield to your desires any longer. I will not act a fool for anyone besides Christ. I will present my body as a living sacrifice Holy unto God. Now give Him praise for your first step to *Renewing Your Mind*!

This may sound silly, but we must look in the mirror everyday and encourage our own selves, know your worth, by not allowing your old mindset take full control of your thoughts. We should never give satan an inch because he will take a mile.

May I warn you that soon after you totally surrender to this virtuous spirit satan will come immediately, like a rushing wind and bring war against your mind. You may face tests you never thought you would face. Test that you felt you have already overcome and passed! You must know in your knower, knower who you are in Christ Jesus. My experience with this foolish mindset took me through many unnecessary obstacles and tests which lead me to write this book. I myself had to listen to instruction and receive knowledge from the Word of God and my spiritual mentors to help me overcome my spiritual battles.

When we go against the wisdom and instruction of God, we're acting foolish no doubt about it. I advise you to get a Strong Concordance and look up the word fool or foolishness and Judge yourself. Nothing like acknowledging our own failure or issues Proverbs 1:7

says the fear of the Lord is the beginning of knowledge but fools despise wisdom and instruction.

By you reading this book shows your heart change, and for that reason I believe that God will honor you and that you will see change in every area of your life. We all know that *repent* means *a change of heart, mind and direction,* time to forsake the old man or foolish woman, so we can receive that new Mercy and Grace God has prepared daily for us. No need to condemn ourselves and hide our struggles making place for satan to bring shame to us. Proverbs 28:13 says, *He that covereth his or her sins shall not prosper but whoso confess, knowledge and forsaketh them shall have mercy.* It's Ok to lift your hands high right where you are and shout. Lord I thank You for new Mercy!!

It's because of his Mercy and Grace we haven't died in our sins and allowed our old foolish ways to destroy us, killing every vision that He has placed inside of our spirit. I advise those who read this book and to share it with your First Lady or Co-Pastor because it is so easy for them to hide behind a Spiritual Mask.

Time to take off your Spiritual Mask: Believers are trained by the word of God not to speak negative words over our lives, which is the right thing to do. But it doesn't mean that we over look the war that's taking place within our mind.

James 5:16 tells us to *confess our faults to another, and pray one for another that we may be healed. The Effectual Fervent (heartfelt) prayer of the righteous availeth much.* No that doesn't mean we go and tell every born again believer our struggles because I've learned by experience that your own brothers and sisters who refuse to change the wicked ways, and turn from their foolish mindset, would take what you've shared personal and turn it around for their revenge. Trust no man but do trust that God will place someone in our lives who will have our best interest. I thank God for my Godly friends and family whom He placed in my life in the right season who held my hands through some of the most difficult times in my life.

Time to Expose Our Worse Enemy...Our Old Foolish Mindset

You may ask what do I mean when I say its time to expose the spirit that's warring against our mind. To expose her is to know her. To know her, is to defeat her and have no fellowship with her. Our old man or foolish woman we left behind wants power. She wants to have control over our flesh. We must denounce her like we have done satan the day we left his kingdom and came over to the Kingdom of God.

We must understand and believe that sin no longer has power over us. *Roman 6:11 says reckon ye also yourselves to be dead indeed unto sin, but alive unto God through Jesus Christ our Lord.* No need to fear this spirit if you have the spirit of Christ living on the inside of you, because the anointing in you will individual destroy its works. The only way it could have full control again over us, is we walk away from God and backslide back into the mindset that once had us blinded and lost.

Stop what you are doing right now and declare that..You Are Free from You!!

When this old mindset tries to condemn you remember that we are overcomers in Christ Jesus and that we die daily. Remind yourself daily of what the word says about you in *1 Corinthians 15:31* I protest by your boasting which I have in Christ Jesus our Lord, I die daily! And that the blood of Jesus has forgiven all your past present and future sins.

Never give up on the Holy Spirit in you. Trust Him. *Know that you can do all things through Christ who strengthens you. Phil 4:13.* What a Long suffering Faithful Father We Serve!

We must know that our flesh and spirit are constantly battling time to take this war seriously like never before, so we won't faint in these last evil days, giving satan the trophy he's fighting to win and that's our soul.

Chapter 3

Warring Against One Another!

Let us discuss the battle or war that is warring against our spirit in a way that it would give us a clearer image on how this battle started and the purpose for it. Spiritual warfare is real. We will never be able to put on the armor of God Ephesians 6:11 tells us to *keep on so we will be able to stand against the wiles or tricks of the devil.* Satan knew that Adam and Eve where created by God and that their spirit were just like God and it couldn't be touched. So what did he start tackling? If you say the mind, you are absolutely correct.

Once a believer accepts Christ, their spirit is sealed and protected its perfect just like God. So the only thing that is left for satan to attack are the mind or flesh. Satan knew that all he needed was a place to come inside the minds of Adam and Eve to cause them to walk in disobedience.

Foolish Woman verses Virtuous Woman In Constant Battle:

Galatians 5:17 warn us of this war that's going on in our flesh. It says for the flesh lusteth after against the spirit, the Spirit against the flesh; and these are contrary to one another, so that ye(you) cannot do the things that you would. I love the way the AMP version says, *the flesh and the spirit continually withstanding and in conflict with each other.*

In other words this war that's going on between satan and the believers will continue until Jesus comes and raptures us from this fleshy body! I am a teacher of the word. It's essential to me that you get some wisdom and understanding of this everlasting battle within our mind, so we can live this abundant life Jesus left for us to enjoy. God gave me a revelation years ago concerning this warfare, that has defeated and taken over the mindset of His chosen women and men of God. I had this revelation, but failed to use it for my benefit until I found myself in a spiritual pit and he brought it back to my remembrance to help me escape from myself. God said His people perish, not only because of lack of knowledge, but because they can't bare the temptations and tests that come to try our Faith.

We sometimes perish because we don't know how to use our spiritual weapon during war and don't know how to keep on the whole armor of God. We can't stand with half of our armor, it would be impossible to survive a war and fiery darts without being covered.

The *Helmet of Salvation* covers our head, which protects our mind. Without this protective covering, we will lose every battle of temptation that wars against the mind. We will lose the battle of lust, doubt, fear, depression, oppression etc. We can't fight this battle in our own might. It's impossible but nothing is too hard for God who fights on our behalf. *Luke 18:27 says the things which are impossible with men are possible with God.*

Its impossible to renew your mind without the guidance of the Holy Spirit and meditating day and night on the word of God. Recognizing, acknowledging and experiencing our ungodly thoughts and emotions as they come in will help transform our thinking. Yes, the the battle isn't ours, it's the Lord's but renewing our mindset is our responsibility. You may say, " *Well Tracy, I read and meditate on my word day and night and still see no results.* Well you are not alone, this warfare within our soul (mind) are assigned to keep us focus on the sin or whatever caused the battle, it will never show you improvement. You know that change starts within and works itself outward. We must focus on how Jesus sees us and that's Free and Delivered!

Allow me to go back and analyze in details Galatians 5:17 concerning this spiritual warfare. First of all, it Take two opponents to start a war: We know by our own past experience that it takes more than one person to start a fight or war between each other. Most of us have been in at least one fight in our lifetime. You need to increase a great amount of threats towards one another in order to wage war. In others words, we know what it takes to get on a person's bad side.

Likewise, in the spiritual realm it takes two to start a spiritual warfare within our mindset, we are dealing with two opponents who have been at war since the beginning of time.

Introduction of the two opponents: *Virtuous woman our (new man) and Foolish woman our (old man). Virtuous woman represents our spirit and foolish woman represents our flesh.*

In the next chapter, I will go into more details concerning both spirits.

We know that in every war or fight somebody has to loose and somebody has to win. I am here to tell you that the woman who represents our flesh, will never lay down a red carpet and allow us to win without giving us the biggest fight we ever had.

With this wisdom you are about to receive after reading this book, and knowing that we got the Victory, she stands no chance. 1 Corinthians 15:57 says, *but thanks be to God, which giveth us the victory in Christ Jesus.*

No daughter of the Most High needs to fear her past. She just need to remind herself that she was created to be a Virtuous Woman of God and that she has the power within, to overcome temptation. Temptations that causes her to sometimes yield to her own fleshly desires.

I hear you say, "Easier said than done", winning a fight, sometimes takes focus and determination. If we give up and quit, we will lose every time. *We must calleth those things which be not as though they were Romans 4:27.*

It may look like your old man is winning, but by faith you already got the Victory!

Before I accepted Christ in my life, if someone shared with me that I had an enemy whom is out to get me behind my back. I didn't rush to them and ask if they had an issue with me. Instead I became their so-called friend. I wanted to see who I was coming against just in case something went down!

I believed in the saying KEEP YOUR ENEMY CLOSE.

Praise God! For deliverance from that ugly fighting demon but we still need to know who our spiritual enemies are, so we can get in our set position and be ready to use our spiritual weapon against every demonic activity that is trying to come up against our mind.

The strongholds that we battle with everyday, thats comes from our Unrewned mind, are the reason why so many Christian marriage are broken. In this next chapter, I will talk about a virtuous wife and how God will hold us accountable for how we treat our husbands.

Chapter 4

God's Plans for a Wife is the Same Yesterday, Today and Forever

As a wife, this section of the book has touched me the most. Why? Because it's my heart desire to manifest this virtuous wife spirit and to make my Father smile and husband happy. Marriage is very challenging at times, but not difficult I truly believe that every marriage ordained by God could last forever if we only follow the principles and guidelines in the bible.

As a wife, I've made some bad decision and a few mistakes but I'm happy to say that by the Grace of God I have learned from those mistakes and turned more toward God for my counsel to help me in the areas that I'm weak. I pray those of you who are reading this book desire the same, that God will give you a heart to love and submit to your husband and as He commands us to do.

I have been with my loving husband for 23 years. I can say without pride that most of those years have been fabulous and joyous. I married my best friend, my mentor, my protector and my soul mate. I give God all the Glory for giving me a husband after His heart who loves his family unconditional.

If you are a single woman of God and praying for a husband, make sure you first hear from God before making a decision to marry. You must be ready for the challenges that comes along with marriage. If you have a gift to stay single please do so, because there will be less hindrance during your walk with Christ.

1 Corinthians 7:34 says, *There is a difference also between a wife and a virgin. The unmarried woman cares for the things of the Lord, that she may be holy both in body and in spirit: but she that is married cares for the things of the world, how she may please her husband.*

I love what Paul said 1 Corinthians 7:7-8, *I wish that all were as I myself But each has his own gift from God, one of one kind and one of another. To the unmarried and the widows. I say that it is good for them to remain single as I am.* Single women of God should have no hindrance on becoming a Virtuous Woman unless she refuses to die to self. Singleness should not be called a curse. You should ask God for wisdom concerning marriage. (James 1:5) This is not for those who feel like they can't handle a single lifestyle.

Listen to what Paul has to say in 1 Corinthians 7:9 *But if they cannot have self-control, let them marry: for it is better to marry than to burn with passion.*

Make sure you read this book and apply it to your life on a daily basis so that when you are ready for marriage it should be easy for you to die to that old Foolish Woman mindset. If I had this revelation before I got married, I would have been able to handle challenges and trials in a Godly way instead acting out on my ungodly emotions.

Lets take a look at Gen 2:18 *and the Lord said, it is not good that the man should be alone. I will send him a help mate suitable for him.*

Proverbs 18:22 says, *whosoever findeth a wife findeth a good thing, and obtain favor of the Lord.*

God considers us women as a favor to our husband we should be walking in favor before we get married making it easy for our husband. Our husband shouldn't have to stress about paying bills and anything else because his wife help brings favor to his household by assisting him with everything that's needed to make a happy home. Our husbands has a role to complete. Sometimes being headship takes a lot of work, they don't need us acting like a Foolish Woman who don't understand order to add unnecessary stress.

After reading and meditating on the book of Genesis, it's safe to say that Eve was created a Virtuous Woman. God would never give His Man of God, His first creation, to an immature woman. I shared before it was that same spirit that deceived her in the garden, causing a curse to her earthly daughter's, passing on that same corrupted and deceived mindset unto us.

Psalms 51:5 says *behold, I was shapen in iniquity; and in sin did my mother conceive me.* The only way to die to this deceived mindset is to die to our old foolish ways and yield to this virtuous Godly woman in us.

Characteristics of A Virtuous Wife: Lets continue to meditate on this virtuous wife by reading what the Word of God has to say concerning her character.

Our spouse must know that he can trust and rely on his wife: Proverbs 31:12 says, a *virtuous woman respects her husband, she does him good all the days of her life.*

In others words, a Virtuous Woman is trustworthy and a help mate. If she brings anything that does not line up to the Word of God, she is out of order. I want you to focus on those three words Out Of Order!

Very few women of God can say that they line up with the word of God concerning their husband all the time. You may say. " Well no marriage is perfect and that we all makes mistakes. I would say that you are absolutely correct. But that doesn't change God's word concerning how a wife should submit to their husband.

With the Help of the Holy Spirit and a willing heart we can become this *God idea* of a wife but it takes total surrender to the new man and putting to death our Foolish Woman (old man). Please never condemn yourself. *There is therefore no condemnation to them which are in Christ Jesus, who walk not after the flesh, but after the spirit.* (Roman 8:1)

Make up your mind today that you will walk after this Virtuous Woman spirit until she takes total control of your life. Believe by Faith, she is living on the inside of us and waiting to reveal herself. Speak to this Virtuous Woman in you; let her know that you are familiar with her presence, then don't allow your old mindset take you out of her presence, which could cause you to lose the battle!

I must admit that I am a work in progress. I can sometimes find myself dwelling on ungodly desires, while I should be spending more time meditating on things that pleases God instead. To work on my character I decided to focus on Philippians 4:8. I advise you to do the same, if you find yourself pleasing your old man more than your new man. You never want your old man to get a head start in this race, because it could slow down the process of you yielding to the spirit, making a place for the devil to win. Amen?

Philippians 4:8 says *finally brethren, whatsoever things are true, whatsoever things are honest, whatsoever things are just, whatsoever things are pure, whatsoever things are of good report, if there be any virtue, and if there be any praise, think on these things.*

A virtuous wife always has an encouraging word in her mouth to help strengthen her husband when he's weak. She loves to minister to not only him but to others who she comes in contact with on a daily basis.

As I mentioned in Chapter One, a virtuous wife knows how to handle her finances she seeks her husband's approval before making a purchase and spends money wisely. She's a woman who know how to budget. (Proverbs 31:16)

Finances issues in a household make a place for the enemy to come in and bring stress, strife and bitterness between husband and wife. Most divorces are caused by financial difficulties. If you know you have a spirit of greed, you need to ask the Holy Spirit to help you, because it will rob you from your faith and in trusting God. Remember money is just a *Seed* not your *Source*.

Nothing is lazy about this a Virtuous Woman. She never put anything on her husband she knows he can't bare. She is willing to help him in every area including working if needed. Not saying that it is wrong for a man to take care of his wife, but a husband should not have to go over his budget to satisfy his wife's greed. I can relate to this statement. I've always helped support my husband, but still need more wisdom on how to budget money.

I'm seeking God's wisdom in this area because I don't want to make a place for the devil concerning financial problems, which could lead to adultery. Most women turn to another man for support when they feel that he can't feed they materialistic desires.

The next time you and your spouse have a disagreement concerning finance, please get rid of that foolish way of talking, and ask the Holy Spirit to give you the words to speak. In this next chapter I will discuss with you how a virtuous woman handles herself during a misunderstandings.

A Virtuous Woman does not have a covetousness Spirit: Covetousness means showing a very strong desire for something that belongs to someone else. A virtuous woman stays within her budget. She never tries to keep up with the Jones's, she is content with what she has and has faith that God will supply all of her needs. Amen?

1 Timothy 6:10 says, *for love of money is the root of all evil which while some coveted after, they have erred from the faith, and pierced themselves through with many sorrows.* Lets continue looking at the characteristics of a virtuous wife by taking a look at Proverbs 31:17. It says *she girdeth her loins with strength, and strengthening her arms.* AMP version: *She girds herself with strength (Spiritual, Mental, Physical) fitness for her God-given task and makes her arms strong and firm.* A Virtuous wife strengthening her arms; not in her own strength, but in the strength of Christ; to whom she seeks for it, and in whose strength she goes forth about her business. She never complains that she's tired because she doesn't rely on her own strength.

When we find ourselves feeling weary while doing what God has ordained for us to do in the Body of Christ, it is a sign that we are relying on our own strength. A virtuous woman keeps her body in physical shape and keeps away from stress by total surrender of her whole body, soul and mind to God.

1 Corinthians 6:19 says *What? know ye not that your body is the temple of the Holy Ghost which is in you, have of God, and you are not your own.*

I pray for whoever reads this book that Supernatural Revelation will flow like never before because we know that faith comes by hearing and hearing the word of God.

Proverbs 31:18 AMP version says, *she tastes and sees that her gain from work (with and for God) is good; her lamp goeth not out, but it burns on continually through the night (trouble, privation, or sorrow, warning away fear, doubt, and distrust)*

A virtuous wife keeps her light shining before and away from men (people) she intercedes during all trials and tribulation for her husband and children needs. She never threatens to leave her husband due to financial difficulties or other challenges that marriage may have. She walks in no fear when coming down to taking care of her family.

We should meditate on these scriptures daily and judge ourselves. Get a pen and paper write down and check off on what you need work on. Remember the word of God is like *medicine to our souls*.

Proverbs 16:24 says, *pleasant words are as an honeycomb, sweet to the soul. (Chooser, thinker, feeler) and health to the bones.*

A virtuous or wise wife teaches her children the ways of the Lord. It's okay to start training your daughter on how to become this virtuous wife by living a godly lifestyle before her. I know easier said than done but don't allow her to see your foolish ways during arguments with your husband.

Proverbs 22:6 says, *train up a child in the way he or she shall go and when he or she is old he will not depart from it.*

I am a living witness to this scripture. My children have seen me at my worst, but I'm quick to repent and acknowledge my wrong doing so they will know the difference between right and wrong and how to have a submissive spirit. My husband and I raised them up in the Lord the right way. Sometimes I reap in a good way from my children, by them correcting me in a humble and respectful way when I do something that's not of God.

This doesn't move me at all because I know they will be a awesome spouses one day, just like their oldest brother. It sometimes amazes me how he treats his wife, but it doesn't surprise me because he was raised up by a father who knows how to treat his mother. Glory goes to God, I often share the joy that I have with the way my children have turned out to be. I want you to also enjoy the joy that comes with your whole household saved. It's Priceless!

My children call me blessed like the Virtuous Woman children in the book of Proverbs 31. No, I'm not saying that I have total surrender to her character, but I will not stop until I become her and I pray you have that hunger as well. I don't care what it may look like concerning your children. Never give up on them. Intercede day and night until you see manifestation.

A virtuous wife is a woman of worth and beauty; she has an inner beauty that only comes from Christ. If you are a child of God that qualifies you to say that you are ordained with that same beauty and worth . Amen?

We stay focus and keep pressing towards doing what's right. Yes we all go through the same test; we all must resist our flesh and yield to our spirit who represents the virtuous wife. We can't allow strongholds which I will discuss in the next few chapters, to prevent us from walking in the will of God and in the character of a Virtuous Woman. They should be pulled down and destroyed before they destroy us. Satan uses strongholds to keep us in bondage to this Foolish Woman we once knew.

God has blessed our husband with favor. We should act like we're a Virtuous Woman that has come into their lives. Let's do our part by by living out the will of God by being the best wife a husband can ask for.

In this next chapter I would like to discuss how a foolish mindset will keep us from walking in a submissive spirit, which God has commanded us to do. My favorite saying is that God will not judge us on how people treat us but He will judge us on how we treat people and that's including our husband.

Chapter 5

A Virtuous Woman Knows How to Speak and Seek Wisdom

A wise or Virtuous Woman knows how to speak and seek wisdom from God, a foolish woman keeps talking during dispute, a wise woman understand the power of her words as well her silence. Oh how have I expose this Foolish Woman within me countless of time, during a misunderstanding with my husband and others as well. I had to get my point across, nobody was not going to get the last word sound familiar? Of course it does most women have that issue.

Satan knows that during a heated argument he has a chance to win because we usually makes place for him to do so. Every time we find ourselves in a place or situation that could cause us to yield to this familiar spirit, we must have a word in our mouth to defeat it.

Proverbs 31:26 says, *A virtuous woman speak with wisdom, and on her tongue there is tender instruction.*

It's safe to say that in our relationship, we want others treat us with respect, yet it seems so hard to reciprocate the same toward them.

Learning how to control our tongue is the essence of true Christianity. No foolish or corrupt words comes from the mouth of a Virtuous woman the bible says when she open her mouth wisdom of the word of God comes out. She express herself in a discreet and prudent manner.

This tongue of ours will cause us to hinder our blessing if we not careful. James 3:6 says, *The tongue also is a fire, a world of evil among the parts of the body. It corrupts the whole body, sets the whole course of one's life on fire, and is itself set on fire by hell.* Most of us Christians know that we will be judged of every idle word that comes from our mouth (Matthew 12:36), but yet refuse to repent and obey the word of God during disagreements, especially with our spouse or whom we in a relationship with.

This is a challenge for me as well so I made a decision, that I will at least have a will to change so the Holy Spirit could assist me. My heart desire is to represent this Virtuous Woman in every area. Because I know that *by our words we will be acquitted, and by our words we will be condemned* Matthew 12:37.

The bible says in James 3:8 *that no man can tame the tongue it is an unruly evil, full of deadly poison.* This does not mean that we can't control our tongue, but that it is impossible effectually subdue it.

Lets focus on this word *subdue,* it *means bring somebody under forcible control.* You may say well Lady Tracy I have tried and tried to control my tongue but it gets difficult at times. That's the problem we trust in our flesh to help us which is impossible since nothing good dwells in it. Instead we must learn to rely on our helper Jesus left for us which is the Holy Spirit.

Jesus said, *the things which are impossible for men are possible with God (*Luke 18:27). We must ask the Holy Spirit to help us when we are tempted to say something that's not of God, remember that we represent the Kingdom of God with the words that we speak.

We must know *greater than He that's in us (Jesus) than he (satan)that's in this world* (1 John 4:4) and that *we can do all things through Christ who strengthen us.* (Philippians 4:13).

Jesus is touched by our infirmities (weakness), He know how difficult it is to control the tongue and obey the word of God when the enemy comes to tempt the God in us. He went from judging hall to judging hall but yet said a word, thank God that He is interceding on our behalf. The good news is He overcame every obstacle so those who followed Him could do the same. Amen?

Hebrews 4:15 says, *for we have not a high priest who cannot be touched with the feeling of our weaknesses; but was in all points tempted like we are, yet without sin.*

Jesus walked in the flesh for 33 years He understands the evil that dwell within our flesh, the good news is that sin shall not have dominion over us Romans 6:14. The bible says in Romans 8:12 we all have obligation but it is not to the flesh, to live according to it.

Please know that He would never force us to become a virtuous woman we must be hungry for righteous so He can manifest a Virtuous Woman spirit through us until we overflow with the anointing she carries. Matthew 5:6 says, *those who thirst after righteous shall be filled.*

Ask the Lord to filled us with His precious spirit He can also help us in the area where we weak, from this day forth speak this virtuous woman to existence in your life. Shout, "I am that Virtuous Woman of God because she lives on the inside of me!!"

A Virtuous woman has a quiet spirit: 1 Peter 3:4 says, *but let it be the hidden man of the heart, in that which is not corruptible, even the ornament of meek and quiet spirit, which is the sight of God of great price.*

A Virtuous Woman handle's confusion well, she has a calm, patience, caring quiet spirit during a confusing situation. I once again must admit that I am need of Mercy in this area. I digress for a moment to focus on what is a quiet spirit are so you can get some understanding why it is of importance to God for His women of God to walk in this spirit. Does it mean that we should walk around everyday with our mouth shut and head down? Certainly not! I think our Father created many different kinds of personalities. A woman who is shy and have very few words to say could be suffering with low self esteem, there is nothing quiet in the natural about a Virtuous Woman, she to busy talking about the word. Amen?

God does not give us a spirit of fear but of Love and a sound mind. 2 Timothy 1:7. If our mind become disturbed easily or when we find ourselves getting offended easily, it could be a sign that we are not walking in a quiet spirit.

Greek words translated *quiet* reveals synonyms like peaceful, tranquil, restful and undisturbed. You may ask why should we need instruction to have a restful spirit? Easy because we can get so easily disquieted in spirit.

Disquieted in Hebrew mean to murmur, growl, roar, cry aloud, mourn, rage make noise, tumult, turbulent, be clamorous, to be trouble, to be boisterous and the list goes on.

Now we can see that most women carry a disquieted spirit which is not God's will for our life. How many of us can say that we have felt trouble and even complained or murmur when we should be having faith? Most of us can relate to this familiar spirit.

When I look at the word *clamorous* I am so ashamed to say that I sometimes find myself walking in that ungodly mindset. Lets take a look at the meaning of clamorous: *super loud and obnoxiously crying out.* I can find myself acting clamorous only during a dispute with my spouse, when I don't have my way I get super loud acting like I have lost my mind. I've once or twice boast on how blessed he are to have a woman like me and of course during that time he would look at me with a surprised glare, like, Yea Right!! Where is the Virtuous Woman I married.

You may say well Lady Tracy how can you write about someone you not living? Well its not like I don't know how to manifest her fruit I sometimes choose to obey my flesh like most women in the body of Christ chooses to do. I am no different than many of you. Yes, as a co-pastor and a leader the Holy Spirit deals with me on a higher level writing this has discipline me in away that I have no choice now but to practice what I preach.

My life will never be the same after writing this book and I pray yours won't be the same after reading it. We should ask the Lord to give us a gentle and quiet spirit.

A *gentle spirit* is not contentious (inclined to argue), careless, bitter unstable, troubled, fearful, obnoxious, prone to cursing, quick to get angry, easily dismayed, easily upset, emotionally unbalanced, impatient, doubtful, foolish, abrupt, irritable, proud, insensitive, self-absorbed, self-seeking, over confident, and with a low- self esteem.

Now you see why I say that I am a work in progress just like everybody else in the body of Christ. For some reason people think pastors wives should be perfect and don't need help in this area. Each of us have something we need to pray and ask God to help us with. No woman or man of God should live comfortable without convictions with such behavior.

In the following chapter I will share with you how we should walk in a submissive spirit as a wife and how refusing to submit will feed our old man making it difficult to walk in a Virtuous Woman mindset.

I've added a prayer that I pray daily and I believe that we all should pray from the heart daily asking the Lord to create within us a pure heart that will not sin against Him. Pray this prayer by faith until you see improvement don't allow your current circumstances condemn you to where you don't see yourself changing daily into the mind of a Virtuous Woman.

Father I come to you in the name of Jesus thanking you for this book Foolish Woman verses Virtuous Woman. I thank you as I read this book my life will immediately change as I make a decision to apply the word of God to my life. I thank you Father for a quiet and gentle spirit.

I thank you Father from this day forth, by faith I will not walk in a disquieted spirit. I thank you Father that I am total lead by the Holy Spirit. I shall be called your Virtuous woman of God. None of me All of you Holy Spirit.

I rebuke every demonic forces that tries to come against my mindset. by faith I am dead to my old (foolish) man and alive to my new (virtuous) man. Father you the Potter and I'm the clay, I ask you to mold and shape me into a Virtuous Woman who look just like you. I Receive her this day!!

In Jesus Name Amen!!

Now Give Our Father The Highest Praise!!!!! We on our way to becoming this anointed virtuous woman of God.

Chapter 6

A Foolish Mindset Versus a Submissive Mindset

Now we know how a foolish mindset works lets see why satan war against our mind to keep us from receiving a submissive mindset. The only way we would walk fully in the character and integrity of a virtuous woman we must first know how to operate in a submissive mindset.

Another touching chapter for most of us the enemy know that if we don't submit first to God then our husband and those who has authority over us we will not walk in our purpose. How can I develop this submissive mindset that God commanded me to have how can I submit to my husband when he does not submit to me? The answer to that question is we have got to desire a submissive spirit God will never force anything on His children it's a choice we all must make to be obedient to His word.

God said in Deuteronomy 30 that *he lay down life or death, blessing or cursing and told us to choose.* Even though we been delivered from all curses God still give us a choice to live a life of blessing and only those who obedience will eat off the good of the land. I struggle with this spirit for so many years I didn't want my husband to tell me anything I thought I already knew everything. Rolling my eyes and slamming doors was my way of expressing my unsubmissive spirit. I know what the Bible says about being submissive I just chose when, where and how I wanted to apply this word to my life. During this time I had no understanding that it was *strongholds of rejection* that was taking hold of me. I felt like if I obeyed him, he wouldn't appreciate me anyway, he only would abuse the opportunity I allowed.

We must be sensitive and obedient to walk in a submissive spirit: A Virtuous Woman spirit will never latch out of her husband instead she will walk away with a quiet spirit until her husband calms down. She must be sensitive towards her husband feelings. Most of the time our husband may get upset because he's stressed or overworked. If we can't be sensitive to God by obeying His word because we know that every time we sin we hurt Him. Don't expect that a submissive spirit will overtake us during a heated argument with our husband.

A Foolish Woman is loud. She always have to get her point across and don't care who feelings she hurt. God has given us a spirit of quietness to think about how we should keep quiet when our husband upsets us. It's wrong when we go three, sometimes, four days without talking to him, knowing that would hurt him doing evil for evil and walking in our old foolish mindset we once walked in before our new birth in Christ.

This mindset will not only hinder our blessing but delay our destiny. If God can't trust us to be obedient to our husband He can't trust us with His people who he has called us to minister His word. It takes walking in a submissive spirit to handle the nation. We can't walk away from people who God called us to spread His word just because we can't have our way with our husband.

We must have an intimate relationship with Holy Spirit so He can train us how to become that Virtuous Woman of God who has a Christ like spirit. A foolish mindset will never ask the Holy Spirit for help it will do the opposite instead, acting on emotion. We must ask the Holy Spirit to help us apply what we read and to mold us into a woman who lives a lifestyle of submission. We love to apply the word to our lives if it benefits us but sometimes rejects the word when it discipline us. We need a biblical sense or wisdom of submission so we will not get confused and frustrated when our husband remind us what the word say when he walking in his God given authority.

Oh how that use to burn my heart when my husband corrected me under the anointing because my foolish mindset wouldn't accept or receive his correction. I would tell him, *Don't use God word for your advantage, don't bring the word up in my face preached to yourself!* Whatever it took for me to avoid receiving a submissive spirit, I have done it. But after setbacks I began to examine my lifestyle the way I think, the way I speak. I was fed up with not moving in the things of God. I knew exactly what needed to be done, starting with my husband, I started to turn every negative thoughts about submission into positive thoughts and action.

Took me awhile to receive this submissive spirit but I wasn't going to stop seeking the mind of this virtuous woman until I receive her with my whole heart, soul and mind. Not saying that my flesh don't sometimes want to act out when my husband walk in his authority we as women know that it's a daily process to die to self and our old ways of doing things.

A woman who has a carnal and fleshly mindset can't walk in submission: A woman who has a fleshly or carnal minded spirit can't have a submission mindset towards her husband and God either. Romans 8:5-7 says, *For those who are according to the flesh and are controlled by its unholy desires set their minds on and pursue those things which gratify the flesh, but those who are according to the Spirit and are controlled by the desires of the Spirit set their minds on and seek those things which gratify the Holy Spirit.*

We know by reading Chapter 2 of this book that a foolish mindset will never pursue a submissive spirit because it only want what it want and thats sin. We can't go another day in the Kingdom of God operating in this spirit I don't care how satan turns up the heat in this war that we battling within our minds.

We must let him know today that if it takes all I have in me I will seek those things that satisfy God and I know a submissive spirit are one of those things. Let's lay aside everything that is coming against us from being submissive. We have too much to offer the Kingdom of God and satan knows it.

Tell him you may form your schemes of defeat; But It Won't Prosper!!

Satan know that we as God chosen women must have a submissive mindset that's the only way we will be able to do what Ephesians 5:22 says, *wives be subject or be submissive to your own husbands as a service to the Lord. For the husband is head of the wife as Christ is the Head of the church, Himself the Savior of His body. As the church is subject to Christ so let wives also be subject in everything to their husband.*

We can argue with our husband when he brings up this scripture mentioned, but we can't argue with God's word. His word does not lie, if He said it then we must obey it. Single ladies who are reading this book, make sure you practice on your submissive mindset by being submissive to your boss and all of those who have authority over you, so that when you get married you won't have the struggles like most of us women of God has today.

God want our marriage to subject to Him so he can be in it, He want to be in every part of our lives. A submissive spirit is a key to Holiness don't think satan going to lay down a red carpet for us to walk in this virtuous woman mindset, he don't want God in our marriage especially if it's Holy.

2 Corinthians 7:1 says, *Therefore, since these great promises are ours, beloved let us cleanse ourselves from everything that contaminates and defiles body and spirit and bring our consecration to completeness in the reverent fear of God.*

Satan knows that flesh cannot dwell in the presence of God he doesn't want our marriage to smell good in God's nostril. We represent Christ who is Holy. That old foolish mindset represents satan who is evil. Nothing cute or Holy about us when we walk in a spirit that not submissive towards her husband, think about the looks we give our husband when that old foolish woman show her face then you would agree with me that I'm telling the truth.

If you are saved and your husband is not, you still must develop this mindset and submit to your husband. God's word is for all who reads and it's Holy even to the unbelievers. My husband and I came over to Lord together so I didn't have to live the life with a husband who doesn't believe. But do know that the word of God is the truth and it will set those who living this life free from not being submissive to their husband.

Keep trusting God's word that says in 1 Peter 3:6 that we are no longer Eve's daughters who walk in a corrupt mindset we are the daughters of Sarah who followed her husband Abraham guidance and acknowledge his headship authority over her by calling him lord, master and leader. The feeling I get when I call my husband Pastor since he's my spiritual leader it feeds my submissive spirit and makes me desires it even more.

Don't allow strongholds which I will discuss in this next chapter keep you in bondage from receiving this submissive mindset. So much to share on this subject but I believe it's enough to help you realize how important it is to us and God that we walk in Obedience towards our husband and all those who has authority over us.

In the name of Jesus I speak breakthrough in every area of your life no matter what the enemy say we know that we have the mind of Christ and we will live a life of submissiveness because we have to power and anointing within us that will destroy the spirit of disobedience.

Characteristic of a spirit that's not submissive: Since we desire to become a Virtuous Woman or walk in her spirit I would like to discuss the characteristic of a spirit that doesn't submit. Print and tape these examples on your mirror are where ever you spend most of your time at and read them daily.

Examine your own life because the only person who can change us besides the Holy Spirit is us. Don't allow this foolish woman take away or grieve the Holy Spirit and hinder the anointing on your life by rejecting the truth. Let our Father know that you are willing to change and yield to this submissive mindset to accepting the knowledge that coming from this book.

Lets take a look at the characteristic of a spirit that's not submissive.

A woman who has a controlling spirit over her husband embarrassing him in public and even in his home. Proverbs 12:4 says, *A virtuous wife is a crown to her husband but she that maketh ashamed is as rottenness in his bones.*

A woman who wants to wear the pants rejecting her husband authority, thinking she is wise but doesn't know anything. In fact she is best at tearing down her house. Proverbs 14:1 says, *The wise builds her house, but with her own hands the foolish one tears hers down.*

A woman who knows it all and can't be taught anything, over talking her husband; she has what you call *a take over spirit.* Proverbs 9:13 says *a foolish and rude woman is clamorous she is simple minded and knoweth nothing.* I don't care how much knowledge we gain we shouldn't allow it to stop us from being submissive to our husband .

After looking up the word clamorous in the webster dictionary I knew without a doubt that it's time to change the way I think and run towards the spirit of a virtuous woman. *Clamorous is a noisy, loud and rowdy woman* she thinks by her loud talking her husband would step down from his God authority and bow down to this foolish mindset.

Don't allow strongholds which I will discuss in this next chapter and foolish mindset rob you out of your anointing and relationship with your husband. Put it in its rightful place... your past.

We come to far in our walk to allow something simple as being submissive to keep us from becoming this *idea woman*. God has not given us this kind of spirit He has given us a spirit that think and act like Christ. I advise you to read and meditate on these examples of a Foolish Woman, that way you will cast that thought down and bring it subject to the word of God. We can do this! Nothing's to hard for the Holy Spirit who takes full control of our mind, body and soul.

In the next chapter you will learn how we need what's called, *spiritual desire*, to become a Virtuous Woman. Its time for us to kill every fleshly desires that's been hindering our walk with Christ.

Chapter 7

Spiritual Desires versus Fleshly Desires A Constant Battle Within

Testimony: A while ago, even I felt like turning away from God and giving up hope because of the depths of my despair. I hated myself for not being able to overcome my acting out, yielding to my fleshly desires and saying no to the desires that God has placed on the inside of me. Until I made up my mind that I was going to use the *greater* in me (The Spirit of Jesus) and not allow that old man (my flesh that dwell in my members

(The spirit of Antichrist) win this battle.

God has given me a spiritual desire by placing a vision in me and no devil in hell was going to kill it. I started to yield to my spiritual desires more and dying daily to my fleshly desires. And because *I made that choice* to allow God to shape and mold me into the image of His Son. I saw a transformation take place within me just like Peter, James and

John when Jesus took them up to the Mount of Transfiguration.

God has given His daughters a desires for a purpose and that is to benefit His Kingdom. Without a desire nothing will be accomplished in God. There is an link between our desires and our destiny, and also a link between a virtuous and foolish woman. But this generation of women do not seem to be very desirous of the things of God because most of our desires has been turned into *flesh*. It's time for us to crucify our flesh and die to all fleshly desires and be transformed into the image of a Virtuous Woman.

Desire is a *wish or longing a request or petition*. What are you longing for? What do you find yourself wanting more of? *Desires of the Spirit or Desires of The Flesh?*

This is a very important question to ask because our desires determine our effectiveness in prayer, our intensity in worship and the depths of personal relationship with God. Even satan has a desire: his desire is to turn all of our desire towards him by yielding to the evil that dwells in our flesh. So that he can win us back to his kingdom of darkness. He will do what's needed to keep us in that mindset of a foolish or unwise woman.

If you lost your desire for your First Love (Jesus) and to become a Virtuous Woman, it's not to late to repent and renew your mind back to the things of God. A loss of desire causes us to become careless and slack off in other important ways which could lead to backsliding position. It's *impossible* to follow after the mind of a Virtuous Woman without a desire to be her. When we find ourselves slipping back into a mindset of a Foolish Woman God has freed us from. We need to go back to that mindset when we first believed, when we had a fire for God.

Most of us was full of spiritual desires when we first gave our life to Christ, then when the temptation of the flesh overwhelmed us, we walked away from God and replaced those spiritual desires for flesh. When our flesh tempts us to yield to it. We need to ask the Lord to help us bring our every thoughts under subjection to Him. Our desires should be to have the mind of Christ to help us desire that mindset of a Virtuous Woman, so that we can think her thoughts so that the anointing could flow out through us more forcefully. The Bible does tell us that our *thoughts are not like God thoughts and His plans are not our plans.* But it clearly tells us to *let this mind be in us that's also in Christ Jesus.* (Philippians 2:5)

The enemy will use our minds to create ungodly thoughts and desires just to keep us from moving forward in God. If we allow him to do as he please by yielding to our fleshly thoughts it could lead to destruction. But if we allow the Virtuous Woman in us take over; satan and his kingdom are in for a fight.

God desires to fill us with His desires, everyday He is speaking to the heart of His chosen daughters trying to deposit something into our spirit that would help transform us from that foolish mindset into a wise woman of God. God will only give us the desires of our hearts that He placed within us, no matter how much we pray, decree and declare. God judges the motives of our request.

Most of us prayed this prayer. *Lord give me my heart desires, and quoted Mark 11:24: Therefore I say unto you Whatsoever things soever ye desire when you pray believe that you receive them and you shall have them.* But what's our the motives behind this prayer? Do we pray that prayer to get something spiritually from God or something to help satisfy our fleshly needs? How often do we pray, Lord fill me up with that same spirit of a Virtuous Woman?

In Mark 11:24 God is not talking about materialistic things. He's talking about the desires that He placed on the inside of us to help bring *His Vision* to past. He's talking about *spiritual desires*. But most Christians will take that scripture and request things that only pleasing to the flesh things like money, houses, cars etc.

When God gives us a desire we will know it because our flesh will die to our own fleshly desires: When God gives us a desire we will know it because we die to our own will. It will be more like Lord. *Let Your Will Be Done Over My life*. It's a *desire* that can't be quenched because it comes from the Holy Spirit who fills us with spiritual gifts.

A spiritual desire is a gift from God everybody can have, but only a few will receive, just like *salvation*. I'm sure you feel the same, if not, you wouldn't be wasting your precious time reading this book. I'm sure you are tired of your flesh hindering your walk with God. I'm ready to see manifestation of my new man or that Virtuous Woman in me, and I know the only way that could happen, if I totally die to my will and fleshly desires.

Paul felt the same way, he recognized the evil that dwelled in his flesh and so should we if we desire to become a wise woman of God. Lets take a look at Romans 7:18. *For I know that in me (that is, in my flesh) dwelleth no good thing, for to will is present with me, but how to perform that which is good I find not.* Paul is saying the will to do whats right is in me but sometimes I still choose to yield to my flesh and do what's wrong.

How many of us today use that same excuse? I desire to yield more to God and a Virtuous Woman mindset, but that old familiar foolish spirit that dwells in my flesh won't let me. But I won't give up until I crucify my flesh and become the woman that God created me to be.

If you desire to crucify your flesh write down this scripture Gal 5:17 *For the Flesh lusteth against the spirit and the spirit against the flesh and these are contrary to one to the other so that you can't do the things that you would.* Let the enemy know that you are one step ahead of him and that you will not give up without a fight. Every day we will be tempted with our flesh, we must decrease to our will, so the Virtuous Woman in us can increase. This wise woman in us is willing to do what's right but when we yield to our old man our flesh become weak.

Jesus had all the opportunity to yield to His flesh, but His desires was to please the Father more so He *passed the test.* In Matt 26:41 Jesus told His disciples to *watch and pray that ye enter Not into temptation, the spirit is willing but the flesh is weak.* Amp version: *All of you must keep awake (give strict attention, be cautious and active) and watch and pray that you may not come into temptation. The spirit indeed is willing but the flesh is weak.*

Jesus knew that nothing good dwells in this evil flesh of ours. He needed His disciples to pray for Him while He went up to pray to God concerning the vision God has given Him to save this lost world. Jesus *flesh* did not want to take that cup that He had to *drink* from. Matt 26:42 says, *Jesus went up to Gethsemane the second time and praying saying. Oh my Father, if this cup may not pass away from me except I drink it, thy will be done.*

A *spiritual desire* gives us *hope* to become a Virtuous Woman no matter what our struggles, we will never lose hope that one day we will walk in that Virtuous Woman mindset. Proverb 13:12 states, *Hope deferred maketh the heart sick, but when desires come in it is the tree of life.* When we lose Hope our heart becomes sick causing us to yield more to our own desires, when we yield to spiritual desires, it helps renew our mindset which brings healing to our souls. *Desires accomplished is sweet to the soul : but it* *is a abomination to fools to depart from evil. (*Proverb 13:19)

What's blocking the change in you? What are you yielding to that's hindering your walk with Christ. What sin in you, are you afraid to let go of, that's causing you to reject the only one who can lead you to your destiny.

Flesh can't go with us to our *destiny*, it just won't fit. We must be willing to *die to all fleshly desires and replace them with spiritual desire to become a Virtuous Woman:* If we don't die daily to our fleshly desires we would never walk in a Virtuous Woman mindset. Instead we will continue to walk after a foolish mindset and please our fleshly desires.

I believe, because you chose to read this book that you have a desire to please God and become this Virtuous Woman. We as daughters of God have the power in us to change once we accept Christ, we by faith died to all fleshly desires and sins. I don't allow my weakness dictate who I am in Christ Jesus when I find myself yielding more to that foolish mindset I quickly judge myself by going to the word of God and applying His principles on how I should act as a woman of God.

Lets take a look at Ephesian 2:1-3, *And you hath he quickened, who were dead in trespasses and sins. Wherein in time past ye walked according to the course of this world, according to the prince of the power of the air (satan), the spirit that now worketh in the children of disobedience. Among whom also we all had our conversation in times past in the lusts of our flesh, fulfilling the desires of the flesh and of the mind and were by nature the children of wrath, even as others.*

As I stated several of times in this book, our *flesh* is evil and can only produce evil. Romans 8:7 says, t*he mind of the flesh is enmity against God for it is not subject to the law of God, neither indeed can it be.* It would be almost impossible to read this book, apply it to our lives and walk in a obedience mindset, if we don't put to death our flesh daily by not yielding to it. Yes, our flesh will be tested day and night to see if we are truly who we claim to be, this an everlasting war that we're facing and would take a spiritual desire to win it. Most of us struggle for years due to lack of knowledge and understanding of the *flesh and spiritual* warfare.

But thank God for new revelation, we are now ready to go to the next level in Christ Jesus with a mindset of a wise woman, who know how to overcome every obstacle and temptation. Greater is He thats in us then our flesh which comes from our corrupt nature. Just like we should go from Glory to Glory we should die daily to this flesh. Only God can produce in our soul, spiritual things or Godly desires. Our soul is implanted by the Holy Spirit; we may act like our old man at times, but in reality we are new creature.

2 Corinthians 5:17 says, *wherefore if any man is in Christ there is a new creation, the old things are passed away, behold they all are become new.* The old us or nature is corrupt, our divine nature is pure and holy.

Before I became that mature woman of God. I also yielded to my own fleshly desires. I had no desires for spiritual things of God. I knew something was lacking, something seriously wrong. Finally, I made my mind up to yield to that wise mindset, someone who had wisdom on how to use the spiritual weapon that was needed to win this spiritual battle within. We need to search our heart daily and see what's preventing us from yielding to spiritual desires that God has placed on the inside of every born again believer.

We as women sometimes walk by our emotions and feelings making it difficult at times to yield to *spiritual correction.* We may often feel that paying attention to our desires is somehow selfish and that we shouldn't honor our desires if they are being truly generous with God. To help discipline myself, I wrote down all my fleshly and spiritual desires on a piece of paper and begin to bring my flesh under subjection. I got a vision in my mind that one day my spiritual desires will out weigh my fleshly desires. I knew that I had to be spiritual minded to become a virtuous woman and if I don't faint, my vision would come to pass.

After seeing with my spiritual eyes what I had to die to, brought conviction to my soul. I began to do what the Bible tells us to do and that is to *judge ourselves so that we won't be judged.* I'd rather *work out my own salvation with fear and trembling* by applying the word on my life than to be judged by God.

If we continue to yield to our fleshly desires and continue to disobey God, it could cause us to be turned over to a *reprobate mind. A mindset that's doom for hell because it refuse to change. Faith comes by hearing and hearing the word of God (Romans 10:17).* Discipline comes by hearing the word and acknowledging our wrong doing which gives us a desire to do what's right in the eyes of God.

Write your fleshly and spiritual desires down and get a vision, see yourself free from everything that's not of God in your life. See yourself yielding only to spiritual desires that God has placed on the inside of you. God wants us to have His desires so He can communicate with us. It is impossible for God to talk to our *flesh* because He said, *flesh can't dwell in His presence (Romans 8:7).* He can't minister to our spirit on how to become His idea woman if we don't have a desire to become her. Our deepest desires should be God desires for our lives.

Ask God what do You want me to do? Let Him know that you only desire to be filled with His desire so He can Give you what you ask of Him. God will never fulfill our fleshly desires that pleases our flesh but He will fill us with His desires to do the work of His Kingdom.

Jesus is Asking Us Today Do You Really Want To Become A Virtuous Woman? We can beg and cry blood during our prayer time asking Jesus to change us into a Virtuous Woman, but if we don't show Him that we are ready to change from foolish to wise. He will ask that same question he asked those in the Bible before they received their healing. *Do you want to be made whole?*

Jesus ask the Blind (Beggar) Bartimaeus what do you want me to do for you? Bartimaeus had a desire to see since it didn't go against the word because the Bible says we are *Healed by the Strips of Jesus*! Bartimaeus request was answered and his desires were met. We can't expect God to do something that goes against his word even if our flesh desires that thing. In order to become spiritual minded and desire spiritual things, we should meditate on God's word as chosen women in the Bible who had a mind like Christ. Women who didn't have time for fleshly desires because they was too busy doing what God had called them to do in His Kingdom.

There is one particular woman of God in the Bible name Deborah in Judges Chapter 4. Deborah inspired me to desire to be used by God. I admire her ambitious and courageous spirit to lead God's people. She was not only a prophetess but the only *female* Judge mentioned in the Bible. She lead a successful war plan, to win the battle against Jabin the King of Canaan and his military commander Sisera.

After meditating on Deborah's story in the Bible, my desire to be used by God and become His chosen leader to help His daughters rise up and be all that they can be, grew stronger. When we desire to become a Virtuous Woman, we will find ourselves asking God for spiritual things and wisdom making no room for our fleshly desires to take over.

A few years ago before I accepted my calling. I had to undergo a *major spiritual heart surgery*. I wasn't sure if I was going to come out of this surgery complete and whole. Not that I didn't have faith that God was going to see me through, my faith just wavered a little. I knew I had to do a spiritual heart transplant because my heart were getting sick from fleshly sinful desires that was killing my desires to become a Virtuous Woman. I had to die to Tracy's fleshy desire, so God could fulfill His desires in my life.

When we learn things about ourselves by naming all our fleshly desires it tells us something about who we are. It helped free me from doubts about what I wanted and focused more on God desires for my life. After writing down my Ungodly Desires and comparing it to my Godly desires, I now realize that I'm closer to walking in the mindset of a Virtuous woman than before.

Expressing these desires also brings us into a closer relationship with God. When we tell God our desires, our relationship to God deepen, we also find ourselves obeying and yielding to the Holy Spirit more as He begun to do a work on us to see if our desires are lined up with His perfect will. In chapter twelve I will go in full details on how God shapes and mold us into a Virtuous Woman.

Desire is the primary way that God leads people to discover who they are and what they are meant to do. We were created to be God's idea Virtuous Woman just like Eve, but it was her fleshly desire that caused her to yield to the voice of satan. Eve had a way of escaping that temptation but she chose not to. (1 Corinthians 10:13)

We must be willing to do away with hidden sins that's causing us not to yield to a Virtuous Woman mindset: There are one in particular that I would like to discuss that we sometimes seems to look over in the Body of Christ, the *sin of lasciviousness.* Lasciviousness is a gross form of wickedness that has sexual overtones in many cases. It starts with a sinful heart. In Mark 7:20. *Jesus said, that which cometh out of the man that defileth the man.*

Mark 7:21-22 says. *For from within out of the heart of men proceed evil thoughts, adulteries, fornication, murders. Thefts, covetousness, wickedness, deceit, lasciviousness, and evil eye, blasphemy, pride and foolishness. Jesus said all these things comes from within and defile a man or woman.*

Lasciviousness starts with a sinful heart then manifest itself in our flesh. In your quiet time I advise you to read and meditate on Gal 5:13-24. If we desire to become a virtuous woman but refuses to die to our fleshly desires and acknowledge our hidden sins it would be difficult to do so it will only feed our old foolish mindset giving it power over us.

We as women in the Body of Christ sometimes focus more on our outer appearance, on how we dress in the Body of Christ, then on what's important. Our evil flesh is destroying the character and integrity of God's chosen daughters.

What's in your flesh that keeps you from moving forward in God? Is it one of these sinful acts or something else? Whatever it is, deal with it. Don't hide or deny your weakness. It's okay to admit that you struggle in areas that may be preventing you from walking in the mindset of a Virtuous Woman.

God can't bless us if we cover up our sins, no matter how much we declare and decree we can't prosper. Proverbs 28:13: *He that covers his sins shall not prosper, but whoso confesses and renounces them will find mercy.* It is folly to indulge in sin and pretend that everything okay. I can recall trying to cover my sin and had no inner peace. If we don't acknowledge our sins, our flesh will win everytime.

Remember this important pattern, bondage leads to addiction and addiction leads to strongholds. If strongholds are not cast down and dug by the root, this could lead to a demon, which then need to be cast out. Are you ready to die to all fleshy desires and start yielding to spiritual desires that will do you good and not harm? A desire that will transform you from a Foolish Woman into a Virtuous Woman?

Yielding to our fleshly desires could lead to mental and ungodly desires. Desires for sexual appetite and passion that feed our old foolish mindset. If you struggling with ungodly sexual desires you don't have to. There is hope in Christ Jesus! In the next chapter, I will go over important details on how God can deliver you from desires that are not of Him.

Chapter 8

A Virtuous Woman Must Be Delivered from Ungodly Desires

If we desire to be this Virtuous Woman we must be willing to endure the pain of suffering, to die to self, and commit ourselves not to sin in thought. Wicked thoughts and strongholds is a spiritual mental disease that needs spiritual deliverance. A woman in bondage to mental and sexual desires has appetite and passion only for the things that pleases the flesh, such as fonication, adultery, prostitution and porn etc. This spirit will only use our body to yield to the flesh. A woman of God who belongs to Christ shouldn't desire anything but spiritual, only that which are pure and Holy and Glorify God.

Galatians 5:24 says, *We cannot belong to Christ Jesus unless we crucify all self-indulgent passions and desires.* Most of us desire to renew our mind but don't know the first step we should take to get rid of ungodly desires. So we continue to have ungodly fantasies which also feed our old man or evil flesh.

In order to get rid of those sexual appetites or sexual fantasies which are forbidden by God, we must renew our minds.

Ephesian 4:23 says, *Be renewed in the spirit of your mind; or by the Spirit thats in our mind,* If you are a child of God you have the Holy Spirit who can assist you in every area of your life. We don't have to struggle with mental and sexual desires, there is hope, but we must be willing and ready for change.

My prayer is, that what you learn from this book and with the help of the Holy Spirit, you will be able to conduct yourselves in purity and wisdom. Wisdom that will enlighten our understanding on how a Virtuous Woman carries herself. The word of God doesn't show favoritism, it is written for each and every one of us, including myself. Most of us yield our bodies to ungodly wicked thoughts or fleshly desires at least once in our lifetime. Our position is not to judge another sister in Christ. But we can encourage one another by sharing biblical scriptures concerning sexual desires.

We should have a prayer partner who we could call up at all times, not only to help us pray that need that we desire, but also who can touch and agree with us to stay out of sin. Be honest with your prayer partner let him or her know your struggle, make sure she is sensitive to your feelings and don't have a judgemental spirit. There is power in touching and agreeing Matthew 18:19 says, *Again I say unto you, That if two of you shall agree on earth as touching any thing that they shall ask, it shall be done for them of my Father which is in heaven.*

Never be ashamed of your shortcoming or weakness what you going through you will be surprised to know that your brothers and sisters in Christ going through the same type of suffering or something worse. Satan don't tempt us with nothing that's not common, he once lived in our body and know exactly what it takes to weakening our flesh.1 Corinthians 10:13 says, *There hath no temptation taken you but such as is common to man: but God is faithful, who will not suffer you to be tempted above that ye are able; but will with the temptation also make a way to escape, that ye may be able to bear it.*

God did not give us the spirit of fear but a love and sound or undisturbed mind. 2 Timothy 1:7. We don't have to fear satan attacks against our minds, but we do need to take it into consideration that this attack is assigned to bring us back to that old foolish mindset. A Virtuous Woman has a sound mind she understand the trick of enemy, she's spiritual sober and alert at all times.

In the book of Romans chapter 6:13 tells us *not to offer the parts of our body to sin, as instruments of wickedness, but rather offer ourselves to God, as those who have been brought from death to life; and offer the parts of your body to him as instruments of righteousness.*

God want us to die to this flesh so we would be able to give ourselves back to Him *no flesh can dwell or Glory in His presence.* (1 Corinthians 1:29). Why boast about what God has delivered us from and forget about what we still need deliverance from? If we break one law we have broken them all. James 2:10 says, *For whosoever shall keep the whole law, and yet offend in one point, he is guilty of all.* If we go ahead and die to this flesh by crucifying it, the process becoming this Virtuous Woman wouldn't be difficult.

Every sin starts with a thought or wicked imagination. If we don't cast that thought down it could eventually enter our hearts, and once sin enter our heart, it would be difficult not to act out that sin. Allowing satan to use us like an instrument for his pleasure. When satan uses our bodies it takes away our desire to become a Virtuous Woman .

Once a Virtuous Woman's mind is renewed, she only desire to think of things that pleases God. A foolish mindset only think of those things that please the flesh and satan. We must be aware of the things in our lives that could lead to sinful acts and mental desires. We have the power in us to help control our thinking let's take a look at Philippians 4:8. Philippians 4:8 says, *Finally, brethren, whatsoever things are true, whatsoever things are honest, whatsoever things are just, whatsoever things are pure, whatsoever things are lovely, whatsoever things are of good report; if there be any virtue, and if there be any praise, think on these things.*

Only a renewed mindset represent a Virtuous Woman, she has a strong mind, yes she gets tempted like everyone else, but she knows how to endure temptation and not yield to those ungodly thoughts and imaginations that satan place in her head. We have to overcome this foolish mindset by not accepting satan invitation to please our flesh.

I have listed below, things that could lead to mental desires and wicked imaginations. I had to overcome this mindset also, and if you apply these principles to your life, you will see transformation take place within your own mind. But you must have a *made up mind*, a mind that's ready for change, if you not ready for change you will continue to walk in that same foolish mindset hindering your chance to becoming a Virtuous Woman.

Things That Prevent Us From Walking In The Mindset Of A Virtuous Woman:

Wicked imaginations will prevent us from walking in the mindset of a Virtuous Woman. If we don't walk in the Spirit, satan could feed us with ungodly and wicked imagination. We will find ourselves thinking about sin more than meditation on righteousness. Walking in the Spirit will help kill the wicked imagination or thoughts in our minds.

We can't desire to be a Virtuous Woman and reject the Spirit of God. Walking in the Spirit means we as women of God, allow Him to direct our path, it means getting rid of our own desires and allowing God to lead us toward the path of righteousness.

Galatians 5:25 says, *if we live in the Spirit, let us also walk in the Spirit.* If Christ lives in us we shouldn't fight against His guidance. Jesus understands the evil that dwells in our flesh, He knows that the flesh only desires what is contrary to the Spirit, it will never agree with your spirit to change into a virtuous woman.

Our flesh only desires wicked thoughts, thoughts that feed our old nature. I have not fully arrived to this Virtuous Woman walk, but I am on standing ground. I won't give up until I see her manifest herself, within me. I may not be where I desire to be, but thank God that I'm not where I use to be. I understand, *if I walk in the Spirit I will not gratify the desires of my flesh.* (Galatians 5:16). If we continue to walk in the Spirit and not the flesh, every wicked imagination that exalts itself against the knowledge of God within our minds will be destroyed.

I know how it feel to struggle with wicked and ungodly imagination no woman of God should live in such bondage. *We must count ourselves dead to sin and alive to God in Christ Jesus of evil desires.* (Roman 6:12). We must allow the Holy Spirit to guide us in thoughts, word and deed so we can be all that God has called us to be. Wicked imaginations are thoughts of iniquity a devil's workshop.

Lets see what the scripture has to say concerning wicked imagination. Proverbs. 6:16-19 says, *Wicked imaginations are literally "thoughts of iniquity.* These are the malicious schemes of the heart that have become the devil's workshop. Psalm 2:1 states, *The heathen rage and the people imagine vain things.*

The devil knows, *if I can get her to yield to her ungodly thoughts; I could win the battle. I can win her back over to me, so I can use her in a worse way than before, canceling out God plans for her life.* I don't know about you ladies who are reading this book. But as for me. I refuse to bow down to satan and his malicious schemes any longer to win me back over to the kingdom of darkness. I have a vision and that vision is the live in the mindset of a Virtuous Woman before leaving this world. I choose to represent the Kingdom of God and not the kingdom of darkness.

God has been better than good to me and He deserve my all, including my mind. It's ok to speak into your own life *whatever a wo(man) thinketh in her heart so is she.* (Matthew 12:35)

If we desire to yield to the spirit of a Virtuous Woman and cast down all ungodly thoughts and wicked imaginations *we must keep our hearts with all diligence because out of our heart come the actions of our lives.* (Proverbs 4:23)

Acting out our thoughts prevent us from walking in the mindset of Virtuous Woman mindset. God hates to see his daughters who imagine and invent evil things and not listen to His will or instruction on how to die to self. Acting out on our thoughts delay the process of walking in the mindset of a wise woman. Psalms. 2:1 says, *some become inventors of evil things.* We serve an all knowing and seeing God, so why pretend that we need no help in this area? God knows our every thoughts, we may hide from people, our wicked thoughts temporally, but never from God.

In the next Chapter I will go over different types of strongholds that cause our hearts to be wicked, keeping us in bondage to wicked thoughts, but first allow me to share a few of wicked thoughts that most women battle within. There are several ways we can act out our thoughts. But I would like to share a few that are most common.

Struggling with *lust* or other sexual desires, masturbation could be a wicked thought that battle against your mind.

Sexual fantasies that are not of God. You would think that only single women struggle with this sexual fantasy but it's farther from the truth married woman deal with this as well.

Many say that *masturbation* is not noted in the bible so its not a sin. But God has most definitely forbidden sinful thoughts that accompany mastubation. When a woman or man mastubate they think of something that causes them to arouse and usually it's an ungodly thought or wicked imagination. At that moment they are not thinking of those things thats pure or Holy which leaves our mind open for demonic activities.

We all need to die to self which is sometimes difficult to practice. Denying the temporary pleasure of mastubation, and choosing to not please the flesh is a sign that we are willing to suffer for Christ's sake. Suffering for Christ's sake, means saying no to sin. One ungodly thought leads to another; starting off with mastubation but eventually leading to sexual immorality.

Lust is an emotional force that is directly associated with the thinking or fantasizing about one's desire, usually in a sexual way. If we deny this demon it will create ungodly desires and wicked imagination. Lust has destroyed the character of God's people in the Body of Christ because they refuse to acknowledge there's a problem.

If you desire to die to that Foolish Woman who we left behind you must acknowledge the fact that this spirit of lust is real. Lust shows no favoritism it will knock on the doors of the heart to who ever opens up to it. We were born into lust or flesh desires it, it craves for it like most of us craves for icecream. If you know you need deliverance in this area get some immediately spiritual help. Seek the Lord for deliverance like your life depends on it because it does.

Most of us think that we don't have this ungodly sexual desire because we haven't' committed a sexual sin with anyone. But listen to what Jesus had to say in Matthew 5: 28-29, *But I tell you that anyone who looks at a woman lustfully has already committed adultery with her in his heart. If your right eye causes you to sin, gouge it out and throw it away. It is better for you to lose one part of your body than for your whole body to be thrown into hell.*

3. Last but not least the *Spirit of Rejection* could lead to ungodly imaginations and sexual sins:

God create sex and nothing is unholy about sex but when we use it to please our ungodly desires or use it to help yield to our fleshly desires that's when it become a sexual sin. We know our duties as a virtuous wife and how we should sexually satisfy our husband but most of us refuse to get rid of this spirit of rejection that normally takes place during conflicts or disagreement with our husband. We find ourselves not wanting to give him what we know that rightfully belongs to him, our body.

Open the door for lust and wicked imagination. It is dangerous to deny our husband from sex. A man was created to enjoy his wife without begging for sex. If we don't satisfy his needs it's possible that he would go and find pleasure elsewhere. The spirit of rejection has destroyed so many marriages in the body of Christ. Cor 7:5: (To married Saints) *Do not cheat each other of normal sexual intercourse, or you will expose yourselves to the obvious temptation of Satan.*

It's time to cast down ever Ungodly imagination that prevented us from yielding to a wise mindset. We need to bring every thought into captivity or control. 2 Corinthians 10:5 says, *Casting down imaginations, and every high thing that exalteth itself against the knowledge of God, and bringing into captivity every thought to the obedience of Christ.*

During the time when I was struggling with ungodly thoughts and wicked imaginations *I had to repent and renounce all legal holds and grounds the enemy had over my mind.* I knew if I rejected that, I had a problem and I would lose not only the battle the warring against my mind, but I would never become that Virtuous Woman I dreamed to become.

How seriously are you willing to die to and give up, to become her (Wise Woman)? We can't enjoy the presence of God yoked up with wicked thoughts and imaginations. Ungodly thoughts hinder the voice of God. The Bible says *my children know my voice and a stranger voice they will not follow.* Wicked thoughts will cause us to tune out revelation and wisdom and yield to what our flesh desires (sin).

The only way we would be able to defeat our wicked thoughts by not allowing it to take control of our minds. We must know that by faith we are dead to that temptation that's warring against our thoughts. Pet 2:24 says, *And he personally bore our sins in his own body on the cross, so that we might be dead to sin and be alive to all that is good.* The enemy has won God's daughters back to him because most of them are spiritually fat and lazy. We must be willing to fight and endure until the end. We must be willing to cast down and take authority over *strongholds and everything else that exalt itself against the word of God.* Nothing should stand in our way of becoming God's idea woman.

Chapter 9
Taking Authority Over Strongholds That Our Old Mindset Created!

Strongholds are a satanic power that have taken ownership of our mind and refuse to let go. Satan has created a battlefield within our minds and determines to win the war. Strongholds is a place of domination: Greek word for stronghold is *Ochuroma* meaning same as compound or fortress, the idea is a structure that has been built to protect something to keep something alive or to prevent someone from entering or taking something away.

When we allow our foolish thinking take over our action it could affect how we respond to various situations in life, and they play a large role in our spiritual freedom. Jesus wants us to live abundance life and it is impossible to do so when we are bond with strongholds.

Strongholds are anything that exalts itself against the knowledge of God, anything whether intentional or unintentional. Strongholds will create idols within our mind which are opposed to the knowledge of God. Remember anything that takes the place of God is an idol. 1 John 5:23 (Amp) *Little children, keep yourself from idols* (false gods); from anything and everything that would occupy the place in you due to God, from any sort of substitute for Him that would take first place in your life.

A stronghold of the mind causes us to *rebel* against God which is a sin of witchcraft a controlling spirit that is designed to take control of our mind and keep us from walking in the obedience of God. (1 Samuel 15:23)

I don't care what's coming against our thinking we need to take it serious and start judging that thought especially if it is coming against our marriage and relationship with God. This is not the time to act like we've got all our stuff together. Rebellion is a witchcraft and stubborn spirit. (I Samuel 15:23)

When we were lost living under control of this Foolish Woman we were under the enemy control or witchcraft spirit: our lives were subject to strongholds. These strongholds were constructed for a purpose, they were designed to keep us lost and blind and to help feed our fallen nature.

For we also were once thoughtless and senseless, obstinate and disobedient, deluded and misled we too were once slaves to all sorts of cravings and pleasure, wasting our days in malice and jealousy and envy, hateful and hating one another. Read the book of Titus Chapter 3 it will explain to you what spirit this foolish woman had control of us.

Satan had a plan for us and that plan had something to do with his kingdom and the only way he could bring that plan to pass was to create a battlefield within our minds or soul. Satan's desire is to keep us blind from the Gospel of Christ so we can perish having no hope. 2 Corinthians 4:3-4 says, *If your gospel is hid, it is hid to them that are lost in whom the god of this world hath blinded the minds of them which believe Not lest the light of the glorious gospel of Christ who is the image of God should shine unto them.*

By experience I've learned that strongholds doesn't come overnight there is a pattern that leads to them below I listed a few things that kept me in bondage *to* this Foolish Woman so many years until I made the decision to change the way I think and instead enjoying my own strongholds start casting them down instead.

Have you heard of the saying You Got To Get Sick And Tired of Being Sick And Tired? Well that's exactly how I felt towards the bondage that I entangled myself in. Yes, we know that the bible warns us not to do that, but the strongholds that we war against can care less about the word it only wants to take full control of us so we continue disobeying God.

Have you ever felt bondage to something like you have been slave to? If yes, that means it's time to cast it down and apply the word of God to whatever have you in slavery. Jesus has set us free from bondage it's not his will for satan to have full control of his people no matter how bad it hurts we have to keep pulling down until we feel ourselves breaking loose from every stronghold and demonic spirit.

Galatians 5:1 *tells us to stand fast therefore in the liberty or freedom wherewith Christ hath made us free, be not entangled again with the yoke of bondage.* I love the definition Webster gives for *strongholds*, a *fortified place* or a constructed thought, picture and images that our mind in fixed on to. When strongholds are negative they can produce or birth addictions and bad habits. They are built upon deception and error.

Deception means you have already been deceived or tricked a primary weapon of the devil, deception is a building block for strongholds which could cause us to think in ways that blocks Gods best for our lives and we wonder why we still struggling. The only way we will be able to survive the enemy deceptive, lying spirit that wars against our mind if we wear the whole armor of God.

Ephesians 6:11 says, *Put on the whole armor of God, that ye may be able to stand against the wiles of the devil.* There hope and deliverance for those who are in Christ Jesus but there is a process we must *tear* down strongholds. How to tear down strongholds: Strongholds are birthed and dwell in deceptions which are lies and false beliefs, so naturally the cure is to bring the truth in God's Word on the scene. We rebuke the lies of the enemy, with the word of God.

It was said even by me that demons can't live in Christian hearts, but they oppress us and whisper in our ears. Think how many times we allow our foolish mindset to yield to demonic activities on countless of times. If we want to live a virtuous life as a woman of God we must tear down and submit to the word of God. It's the word only that's going to keep us free from bondage.

Oh how well do I know how it feels to be in bondage and go on like nothing's bothering me. I was afraid to speak out because I was under *people bondage*,worrying if I say something, I would be judged as a Christian and nobody would look at me the same way. Most Christians think just because they have turned their lives over to the Lord and had the Holy Spirit come into their lives, they are ok, no tearing down strongholds are necessary.

The Holy Spirit is our spiritual aid. He assist us and bring God's word to remembrance in our lives. He will never tear down our strongholds for us, if so, the bible wouldn't tell *us* to cast them down. Satan loves this mindset, because he has a good chance of wrecking our mind, and if he could our lives. I don't know who reading this book, but as for me I am ready to do away with every demonic spirit in wicked places, including my mind so I can walk out the calling the set before me.

Don't allow satan to win this war by keeping us in bondage. We deserve this carefree and abundantly life Jesus gave us. As I will discuss in this next chapter strongholds will lead us to a rebellious spirit against God. Its impossible to represent a Virtuous Woman with a rebellious spirit but it wouldn't be difficult to satisfy our old foolish mindset because it survives from feeding on rebellion.

Before I end this chapter I would like to add a pattern a mighty man God shared with me during a conference concerning strongholds. I took some notes but didn't apply them to my life until later, when I was in a bad place, dealing with my own spiritual struggles.

Strongholds birth babies and if not careful they will also birth demons: Here's a list of strongholds that most of us in the Body of Christ struggle with or has struggled with. We find ourselves praying to God asking Him to deliver us from our infirmities or weakness but seem to forget about the strongholds that are causing us to yield constantly to our fleshly desires.

Stronghold of Bitterness birth: A rebellion spirit, frustration, a self will spirit, hopelessness, distraction, stubbornness, selfishness, a spirit of greed, anger and spiritual blindness or you can say an unteachable spirit. We can't expect to get rid of anger, wrath and slander if we don't kill the root of bitterness that comes from our past troubles. Some women become bitter if they can't have children, if their husband or boyfriend betrayed them and walk out their life unexpected. These are some reasons why we hide bitterness deep within us, not knowing that it would birth other issues in our lives. Hebrew 12:15 says, *Looking diligently lest any man fail of of the grace of God; lest any root of bitterness springing up trouble you, and thereby many be defiled.*

Let's take a good look at two of the spirits that the *stronghold of bitterness* birth, so we can see the root of our problem, and deal with them once and for all. We can't get rid of distraction, stubbornness, selfishness, etc. and ignore the spirit of a rebellion and frustration.

A *rebellious spirit (manipulation)* is as sinful as witchcraft 1 Samuel 12:23. a controlling stubborn and unkind spirit that has more love for the world than others. If you see yourself walking in this mindset, cancel this one out immediately. It can only lead to one thing and that's destruction. In the next Chapter, I will go in further details on how this spirit has prevented Christians from receiving their spiritual inheritance.

A *frustration spirit (anger)* is a person who gets upset and annoyed about things that they can't change or achieve. This spirit will sometimes become angry and do whatever it takes to get what it wants. This person has a unteachable spirit, just like a person with a rebellious spirit which could lead to spiritual blindness.

Stronghold of Jealously: Births *pride,* a spitefulness and vanity and gossip spirit, betrayal, self-centered, critical spirit, judgemental spirit, insensitivity, a spirit that's always suspicious, a resentful spirit, a spirit that's violent and always seek revenge. The *spirit of pride* is a very serious spirit that need to be dealt with and should not be taken lightly. I hate this spirit because it almost cost me my Christianity. The meaning of *pride* in the Webster's dictionary is *a high or inordinate opinion of one's own dignity, importance, merit, or superiority, whether as cherished in the mind or as displayed in bearing conduct.*

The *spirit of pride* in this generation has corrupted mindset of God's chosen women. Pride is one of the reason why most of us don't want to die to our own self-centered and judgemental ways. It would be difficult for us to yield to spiritual things and the Holy Spirit if our heart is corrupted with pride. We can't attempt to die to (the spirit of pride), if we can't admit or acknowledge that we have spiritual struggles. *Stronghold of Heaviness*: Birth Sexual impurity, depression, lust, despair, seductiveness, self pity, masturbation, a forncation and adultery spirit. Before we can cast down a *spirit of heaviness* we must first know what it is right? It's *a feeling of being dull, a spirit that will weigh you down mentally, a sense of fear and failure a very lonely feeling.* This spirit usually comes from low self-esteem that most women struggle with today. I dealt with a spirit of heaviness. I saw the effect that it had on me and I wasn't going to bow down to it's deceiving spirit any longer. I saw myself yielding to the lust of my flesh and turning away from things that's pleasing in the sight of God.

Most of us can relate to this spirit of feeling lonely and weighed down at least once in our lifetime. A *stronghold of heaviness* birth sexual impurity a stronghold, that has taken control of the mind of many women in the Body of Christ. If we don't cast this stronghold down it could lead to lust, fornication and adultery which is not pleasing in the sight of God. No one perfect but Jesus but God still expects for His called out women to respect their body which no longer belongs to them. He want us to abstain from sexual impurity and other issues that the stronghold of heaviness birth.

Lets take a look at 1 Thessalonians 4:3-5 says, *For this is the will of God, even your sanctification, that you should abstain from fornicaton. That every one of you should know how to possess his vessel in sanctification and honour. Not in the lust of concupiscence, even as the Gentiles(unbelievers) which know not God.*

Stronghold of Insecurity: Births a spirit of rejection, lack of trust, feeling unworthy, shyness, withdrawal, compulsions, people pleaser and not God seeker, wrong relationships. A woman who has a stronghold of insecurity lack confidence, she doubts herself in everything she puts her hands on. This spirit comes from past rejection, or lack of support from loved ones. If this spirit is not dealt with it could lead to feeling of unworthy and withdrawal, we see this spirit most in shy women. God doesn't want us to rely on ourselves more than we rely on Him. James 4:10 tells us to *humble ourselves before the Lord , and He will exalt us in due season.*

Stronghold of Control or Jezebel Spirit: Births manipulation, desires for recognition, and sometimes misuse of scriptures. This spirit has a difficult time receiving from others especially spiritual counsel.

Satan is in it, to win it! Now is the time to pull down the spiritual demonic babies or issues and abort them by killing the root of the strongholds. If we don't acknowledge the problem it can't be solved. We are on this battlefield together, why not encourage one another to keep the faith.

This book is written to encourage not only the readers but myself as well, don't give up on yourself. My prayer is that every strongholds we're struggling with, be destroyed and done away with. We know that a foolish mindset will lead to a rebellion and evil spirits that don't have a desire to become a Virtuous Woman.

In the next chapter I will go in further details on how strongholds have corrupted the mindset of many believers. Only you know what strongholds you are dealing with. After reading about these strongholds, judge yourself, then seek God for deliverance.

Chapter 10

A Foolish Mindset with Strongholds Leads to a Spirit of Rebellion

Years ago, I taught this message in my church, and it changed our lives I pray as you read this chapter it would do the same for you. I pray that if you are allowing your corrupt mindset to hinder your spiritual inheritance, you will change the way you think and receive everything that God has laid out for you. I believe that many Christian's today are asking God. Where is my spiritual inheritance and how can I walk in my destiny and purpose?

A Foolish Mindset and strongholds will delay your spiritual inheritance: Now that I've shared with you the importance of casting down strongholds in a previous chapter, allow me to enlighten your understanding in this next chapter about spiritual inheritance. Satan knows that if I can keep God's women and men in bondage in their mind, they would never receive what God has preordained for them to have which is their spiritual inheritance.

Spirit Inheritance is a portion that God had laid aside for his children through Christ Jesus, but we will not be able to inherit it unless we have a leader in our life. Before we could become a Virtuous Woman we should have a spiritual mother who has a Virtuous Woman mindset who can impart into our lives. A spiritual mother who we can look up to, who can spiritually rebuke us when we are out of order, or when we are walking in disobedience. A woman of God who understand the character of the Virtuous Woman and has her mindset.

I thank God for my spiritual mother Edna Hooks she understand her task as a spiritual mother, leader, natural mother and wife. I can recall first hearing her speak and her humble spirit touched me in a way I can't explain, I knew that I wanted the same mindset she had.

Spiritual Inheritance is a portion that God had laid aside for his children through Christ, but we will not be able to inherit it unless we have a leader in our life. Operating in a foolish mindset will allow us to reject leadership which lead to our destiny. It took me a while to get to that mindset to receive spiritual rebuke, but I knew I had to submit to authority if I wanted the blessings of God over my life.

I thank God everyday for my spiritual leaders who taught me the word concerning leadership.

Likewise my husband Pastor Larry Mitchell. I must submit to his authority as well. You should pray for a submissive spirit in this area. Ask God to give you a teachable spirit, whatever your man or woman of God need to assist them in their vision, do your part to help them fulfil it. A virtuous woman don't have a problem submitting she understands authority.

Not saying that being submissive to leadership won't be a challenge, satan will do his part by trying to cause you walk in disobedience. He loves confusion. If you're struggling in this area of submitting to authority, repent quickly and get back in your rightful position as a lay member or leader. If we can't receive a teachable spirit it would be difficult to die to our old mindset and receive a Virtuous Woman spirit.

I see so many women in the Kingdom of God including those who left from under my husband and I leadership due to a rebellious spirit, trying to wear a mantle they had not earned. In others words how can you have your own unless you been faithful unto another man. How can you have your own ministry yet didn't serve another man vision.

Luke 16:12 says, A*nd if you have not been faithful in that which is another man's, who shall give you that which is your own.* I don't care how anointed you claim to be or virtuous you may think you are, without a spiritual mantle you could be walking in a familiar spirit that's leading you down the wrong path.

This a very touching subject to discuss because so many of Christian's today, just don't have the spirit to serve and receive their spiritual inheritance so that they can be all that God has called them to be. They have a hard time listening to another man or woman of God's instruction.

I've listed a few qualification that we must go by to receive the mantle to get us to our destiny and live out our purpose here on earth. Please write them down and make sure that you are operating in a right spirit and not a familiar spirit. These are the qualifications needed that I've been taught and that are Biblical to receive your spiritual mantle and spiritual inheritance.

1. You must be in Christ Jesus; an unbeliever can't receive spiritual mantle or become a Virtuous Woman because it's foolish to them. 1 Corinthians 2:14 says, *But the natural man or woman receiveth not the things of the Spirit of God: for they are foolishness unto him or her, neither can he or she know them, because they are spiritually discerned.*
2. You must have a Spirit of serving, there's an anointing that comes from serving that a lay member who just set on the church pew and do nothing will never get. There's a price to pay for the mantle, being slothful will slow down the process. So many of us want the anointing but don't want to do what it takes to receive it.
3. Impartation of gifts from your man or woman of God, if you are serving under leadership, don't leave without your spiritual inheritance, your inheritance

ties into your destiny. Make sure your spiritual leaders impart spiritual gifts into your spirit which is needed to carry out your purpose. It was biblical in the book of old and likewise for us today. Paul imparted spiritual gifts into his spiritual son Timothy, so that he could fulfil his purpose or calling.

I pray that when it's time for the anointing on your man or woman of God fall, that you will be in your rightful position to receive your mantle. So that you can become God's idea woman on this earth and be all that He called you to be. Serve your leader no matter what comes up against your emotions, don't allow others to talk you out of receiving your inheritance.

I can remember getting upset with my spiritual leader who birth me Pastor Johnny Davis. Since he was my blood brother, I thought I could get away with things others in the ministry couldn't. I felt like I was in High School again because I stayed in the hot seat or spiritual principle's office. Thank God my pastor didn't show favoritism, and walked in his God given authority because otherwise, I wouldn't be the woman of God I am today.

Lets take a look at few other men of God in the Bible who transferred their anointing to their spiritual children. Moses transferred his anointing to Joshua by the laying of hands impartation and so did Paul to his disciples. I'm not saying let everybody lay hands on you because we see in the word that unwelcome spirits will enter by laying of hands.

We should always pray before choosing a spiritual leader to make sure their spirit is from the Lord. Not saying that they must be perfect because that would be impossible since no man is perfect but Jesus. Not everybody who ministers the word is sent and called of God. 1 John 4:1 says, *Beloved believe not every spirit but try spirits whether they are of God, because many false prophets are gone out into the world.*

Last but not least even Jesus who was without sin received His inheritance when He went into Jordan and was baptized by John the Baptist. Read Luke 3:21-22. Jesus knew the importance of spiritual inheritance and mantle because he gave spiritual direction and instruction on how to lead His people.

If we don't allow our virtuous spirit or mindset take over in the Kingdom of God we will allow our old foolish mindset rob us out of our inheritance that God has predesignated for us to have. Don't allow this war that's fighting against our mindset stop you from receiving the mantle that will not only change your life be others as well.

Be real or honest with yourself. We can fool man but not God, He looks at the heart to determine if they are ready for their portion of their spiritual inheritance. If you are serving in a ministry to please man you will never receive your portion that way. Colossians 3:22 tells us to *obey in all things your masters according to the flesh not with eyeservice, as men pleasers but in singleness of heart, fearing God or respecting Him.*

It could have been me but thank God that I made my mind up to walk in obedience because some Christians don't receive their spiritual inheritance because they rejected or rebelled against their leaders authority. You may ask, Tracy how do you know if you are walking in a rebellious spirit? When we choose to obey or yield to the flesh and talk against what those who have authority over us, is a sign that we walking in a rebellion mindset.

Rebellion means an outbreak against authority, this spirit causes us to walk after our own thoughts and not the instruction of God, and those who has spiritual authority over us. Ladies, we can have a problem in this area, because we don't like to be told what to do, but allowing this mindset to take control of us, could lead to a spiritual disaster. It's time to get our act together.

This spirit will have us acting like Judas when he rebelled against this man of God Jesus. Judas walked after his own thoughts. But, like most anointing leaders today, they often recognize the spirit before it acts out. God will place a man or woman of God in our life, to watch over our souls and give us instruction and revelation on how to get or receive our spiritual inheritance. But a person who walks in a rebellious spirit will not hearken to those instructions. They will continue to sin and pretend that all is well with their soul. Isaiah 30:8-9 says, *For this is rebellious people, false sons, sons who refuse to listen to the instruction of the Lord.*

If we choose to follow after a foolish mindset it could cause us to walk away from God and become a castaway. I love the story of the Prodigal son, a great lesson for me. This is an example for us, about a child who abandons a spiritual leader and God to venture into a place where God didn't call him or her. When that happens that child of God will end up walking in a foolish mindset and miss out on their spiritual inheritance, if they refuses to change the way they think ,or renew their mind, and come back to their senses like the Prodigal son did. Satan wars against our mind, because our mind tell our flesh what to do. Speak to your flesh. Tell that foolish woman that you've outgrown, that you will not allow her to cause you to walk in a rebellious spirit any longer, and that you choose this day to receive your spiritual inheritance.

Let the enemy know that you choose to win this fight that's warring against your mind. Let him know that you were born to win and was ordained by God to become a Virtuous Woman. Let him know that you will not give up until the Potter shapes and mold you into the image of God's Son our Saviour Jesus Christ and His idea woman.

We can't do nothing without God's help, even if we try. In order to receive our inheritance and mantle. We must have the mindset to be able to handle this type of anointing. The only way that would happen, if we lay humbly and willing in the Potter's hands and allow Him to shape and mold us into the woman of God He created.

Chapter 11

God is the Potter and We are the Clay

This chapter will show you a side of God that will change the way you see Him. God is the potter and we the clay, it's time for His daughters to lay in the palm of His spiritual hands and allow Him to shape and mold us into His idea woman. Only God can create within us a new heart and transform our minds from unwise to wise. God is our Creator and He has a plan for us that only He can bring to pass. Our life is not our own God is in charged of our life. We been bought with a price it's time to take our hands off our life and allow the Potter do His task.

As I have already discussed in this book, God had a vision or idea for His children. He had a plan for his daughters and sons to be Holy. But that would be impossible without a renewed mind. Let's take a look at the first human created by God, who was Adam.

In Genesis 1:26 *God said let us make man in our own image* (a picture in God's mind). In Genesis 2:5-6 God began to form that man just like He imagine in His mind. God had a vision for His children. He knew exactly how He wanted to shape and mold them into. A child who looks and thinks like Him. If we read down further in the book of Genesis, He later created Eve the first example of a Virtuous Woman of God from the rib of Adam.

God knows the plan he has for us, before He formed us into our mother's womb. Listen to what He told Jeremiah. Jeremiah 1:5 *Before I formed thee in the belly I knew thee, and before thou camest forth out of the womb I sanctified thee, and I ordained thee a prophet unto the the nations.*

He knows the number of hairs on our head (Matthew 10:30). Nobody on this earth including our parents or husband know us like our Heavenly Father. Our Father knows and understand our struggles as well as our weaknesses. He also knows our heart, He knows if we truly want to be transformed into a Virtuous Woman. We can fool man, but never God.

God has called us with a Holy calling, no need to fear change. He will guide us every step of the way. We should embrace change like you would a man we in love with. Never let it go until transformation takes place. God see's us a finish work. We don't have to work so hard, all He ask of us is to stay on the Potter's wheel and He will do the rest.

Hebrews 4:3 says, *For we which have believed do enter into rest, as he said, As I have sworn in my wrath, if they shall enter into my rest, although the works were finished from the foundation of the world.* Glory to God we can shout with joy that it is finished! By faith we are that Virtuous Woman of God who our Father created before the foundation of this world.

I don't care how hard it gets or how many times you feel like giving up on becoming a *wise woman*. Don't give up or faint. If God was there for Jacob and all His children in the Old Testament, likewise He be there for us. Isaiah 44:2 T*hus saith the Lord that made thee, and formed thee from the womb, which will help thee, Fear not, O Jacob,my servant, and thou Jesurun, whom I have chosen.*

You may think that you don't have what it takes to be a Virtuous Woman or it would be impossible for God to change you into the image of His son Jesus Christ. We serve a miracle working God. I love what Ecclesiastes 11:5 says, *As thou knowest not what is the way of the spirit, nor how the bones do grow in the womb of her that is with child; even so thou knowest not the works of God who maketh all.*

God will deal with His children. If they act like they have forgotten who He really is in their life. I'm a living witness to this truth. In the Old Testament God had to deal with a stiff neck nation who refused to change. He will do whatever He has to do to get us to understand His authority and power over us.

God desires to teach us how to be a Virtuous Woman through the Holy Spirit but we must be willing to listen to His instruction.

Listen to God's instruction He gave us in the book of Jeremiah. Lets take this word into consideration, if we get on the Potter's wheel and allow Him to work on us inside and out it would not be that difficult to yield to the example of becoming a Virtuous Woman.

Jeremiah 18:1-6 says, *The word came to Jeremiah from the Lord, saying, Arise, and go down to the potter's house, and there I will cause thee to hear My words. Then I went down to the potter's house, and, behold, he wrought a work on the wheels. And the vessel that he made of clay was marred in the hand of the potter: so he made it again another vessel as seemed good to the potter to make it. Then the word of the Lord came to me, saying , O house of Israel, cannot I do with you as this potter? saith the Lord, Behold, as the clay is in the potter's hand, so are you in mine hand, O house of Israel.*

In Jeremiah 18:3, I love how Jeremiah breaks down the Potter's wheel. It gives us revelation and instruction. He teaches us the power of God and how we should stay on His spiritual wheel, and allow Him to shape and mold us into His image. God desires to shape and mold us into a virtuous woman but the question is. Are we willing to get instruction on how to be a Virtuous Woman whose after God's heart?

Jeremiah 18:4 leads us to the realization and awareness on how our Heavenly Father *puts us on His wheel to shapes us as seems good to Him*. God knows what we can handle and what we can't, He will never allow anything including temptation slip up on us, that we can't bare. All He need is a willing heart and yielded vessel towards Him so He can freely shape and mold us.

Allow me to explain in the natural what the role of a potter is, so you can understand the Power that holds us in the palm of His Hands. A potter in the natural is his vocation or task, he makes vessel or utensil for a living such as vessel pot, spoon, fork etc. I advise you to visit Google.com or Youtube.com and research a potter's task and watch how he handles the clay, it would give you revelation on how God shaped and molds us into a fine creation.

Before the potter begin his task he has in mind or an image on how he would like for the product to turn out (Amen) his goal is to have a perfect product to place on display. Let's talk about one of the products that is Biblical, that we can relate to, such as a vessel pot.

Material needed for a vessel pot is clay, water, wheel, furnace (heater). God consider us a earthly vessel. Hebrew 9:20 says, *Moreover he sprinkled with blood the tabernacle and all the vessel of the ministry. God wants us to know that He has all right over us (the clay) just like the potter have all right or control over the clay.*

After that word that came forth in Isaiah 29, Isaiah realize that we are work in progress. I pray after you read this scripture you too will realize that you are a work in progress. We need to allow our Father to freely shape and mold us and stop fighting His hand and totally yield to Him like it's our last hope.

Isaiah 29:15-16 says Woe unto them that seek deep to hide their counsel from the Lord, and their works are in the dark, and they say, Who seeth us? and who knoweth us? Surely your turning of things upside down shall be esteemed as the potter's clay: for shall the work say of him that made it, He made me not? or shall the thing framed say of him that framed it, He has no understanding?

God understand that we too, need some work done on us, before we can be transformed from a foolish unwise woman into a wise virtuous woman. We must first acknowledge and admit that we need some work done on us, hiding our sins causes us to slip out of the hands of God. We are the work of His hands Isaiah 64:8 says, *But now O lord thou art our father we are the clay and thou our potter and we all are the work of thy hand.*

We quote Corinthians 6:20 *For ye are bought with a price, therefore glorify God in your body, and in your spirit which are God*'s. But do we believe it? Do we truly understand, that it will take some dieing to self and totally surrender to the one who purchase us back from the power of satan. The one who called us out of darkness into this marvelous light.

There's two type of vessels the bible talks about, a *vessel of honor and a vessel of dishonor*. God want us to be His vessel of honor, someone He can shape and mold into His image and send out into this world who represent His Godly character. Someone who He can proudly call His child. Jesus made God proud to call Him His son and we should make Him proud to call us daughter.

Virtuous Woman Represent Vessel of Honor and The Foolish Unwise Woman Represent the Vessel of Dishonor: God's goal is to make a sanctified vessel out of us, but it depends on how we submit and stay humble during the process of Him shaping and molding us. If we get off the wheel too soon and turn away from God, it could cause us to go back out into this world and become once again a vessel of dishonor.

It was said to be careful what you ask or pray for because it may happen. I can recall praying this prayer everyday over my life when I first gave my life to Christ. I had the zeal but no revelation. My prayer was. Lord shape and mold me into a vessel of honor. Holy Spirit help me to die to the things that causing me to be a vessel of dishonor. Not understanding the power of prayer at that time, God heard my cry and the progress begun.

How do I know? Because I had to endure test and temptations that only the Holy Spirit and God could delivery me from. I quoted. Greater is He that's in me, than he(satan) that's in this world, maybe a 100 x's a day. I didn't realized that God was answering my prayers that I prayed years ago, until I felt the war that was taking place within my soul. I knew then that just because I was a Christian and go to church every Sunday doesn't make me a vessel of honor, it takes some yielding to the Potter's Hands.

The bible stated that in the body of Christ we have vessel of honor and dishonor. I wasn't going to give up until I become that virtuous woman who represent a vessel of honor. Read what 2 Timothy 2:20-23 it will explain what type of vessel in the body of Christ.

2 Timothy 2:20-23 says, *In a large house there are articles not only of gold and silver, but also of wood and clay some are for special purposes and some for common us.* Those who cleanse themselves from the latter will be instruments for special purpose, made holy, useful to the Master and prepared to do any good work. Verse 20 is saying *flee the evil desires of youth and pursue righteous, faith, love and peace, along with those who call on the Lord out of a pure heart.* Verse 23 tells us not to deal with anything that has something to do with *foolish and stupid arguments, because you know they produce quarrels.*

God no longer want us to desire foolish and evil things that our flesh desires. He want our whole heart, soul and mind. If we feel Him chastening us count it all joy, because our Father only chastise those who He love and haven't given up on. Most of God's women have turned their backs on Him, giving Him no choice but to turn them over to a reprobate mind, because they refused to hold on to the Potter unchanging hands.

I Refuse to walk in a disobedience Spirit and fight the hands of God and be turned over to a reprobate mind. A mind that's doomed for life. A mind that no longer cares about the things of God. If I didn't make that choice to receive my Father corrections and rebukes, I wouldn't be here today and wouldn't have the wisdom to write this book. Lets take a look at two encouraging scriptures that would explain the love our Father has for us.

Hebrew 12:5-6 says, *God chastens those He love.* And have you completely forgotten this word of encouragement that addresses you as a father addresses his son? It says, *My son, do not make light of the Lord's discipline, and do not lose heart when he rebukes you, because the Lord disciplines the one he loves and he chastens everyone he accepts as His son.*

Go ahead and receive your rebuke and correction, lay in the Potter's hands and take it like a mature saint. Don't give up on your vision on becoming a Virtuous Woman of honor. No chastening feels good to our flesh, but it will be all worth it, when we see manifestation of holiness.

Hebrews 12:10- 12 says, *For they verily for a few days chastened us after their own pleasure; but he for our profit, that we might be partakers of his holiness. Now, no chastening for the present seemeth to be joyous, but grievous: nevertheless afterward it yieldeth the peaceable fruit of righteousness unto them which are exercised thereby. Wherefore lift up the hands which hang down, and the feeble knees.* When we lay on the Potter's wheel and allow him to shape and mold us into a Virtuous Woman and receive His rebukes and correction. When it's time for Him to place us in the fire of tests, we will come forth as gold. Job 23:10 *But he knoweth the way I take when he hath tried me, I shall come forth as gold.*

I understand now, why our Father consider His virtuous daughters more precious than *rubies.* It's because they have proven themselves to be a vessel of honor. They passed tests after tests, endured trials and tribulation. A vessel that stayed on the potter's wheel, a vessel who yielded to God and His ways no matter how high the heat was turned up, when she went through the fire. She was once vessel of dishonor who has been transformed into a vessel of honor.

If you going through the fire and your character and integrity are been tested, Don't you dare give up without a fight. Press through the pressure, know that this is only a test to see if you are ready to become a Virtuous Woman. To see if you ready to die to that old foolish mindset. That same mindset that cause you to get off the Potter's wheel. That same mindset that will cause you to keep taking that same test until you pass it.

1 Peter 1:6-7 says, *Our faith are tested during the fire. Wherein ye greatly rejoice, though now for a season, if need be, ye are in heaviness through manifold temptations. That the trial of your faith, being much more precious than of gold that perisheth, though it be tried with fire, might be found unto praise and honour and glory at the appearing of Jesus Christ.*

Don't grieve the Holy Spirit during the process of Him shaping and molding us by rejecting His help. We are God's *treasure* and peculiar daughters. It takes work to die to this flesh and allow God to shape us into His image. But thank God our spirit needs no work because it has been sealed and is perfect like God. Ephesians 4:30 says, *And grieve not the holy Spirit of God, whereby ye are sealed unto the day of redemption.* Psalms 135:4 tells us that *the Lord hath chosen Jacob unto himself and Israel for his peculiar treasure, and we know that our Father shows no favoritism.*

Don't allow your flesh condemn you and satan either, we all a work in progress nobody has room to boast. We been grafted into the Kingdom of God by His Grace and Mercy. We're not only God's daughters but a royal priesthood, and Holy nation. We were called to be a virtuous Holy woman of God.

1 Peter 2:9 *But ye are a chosen generation a royal priesthood, and Holy nation as peculiar (special people) that ye should show forth the praises of him who hath called you out of darkness into his marvellous light.*

A woman who purge herself from evil works or sins shall be a vessel unto honour, but if she continue to walk in the flesh and fulfil the lust of it shall be a vessel of dishonour. 2 Timothy 2:21 says, *If a man therefore purge himself from these, he shall be a vessel unto honour, sanctified and meet for the master's use, and prepared unto every good work.*

I know how it feels to be tested and thrown into the fire, everybody can't handle the heat and pressure from God's Hands. I know the consequences that we will pay, if we decide to walk in disobedience and reject God's correction and rebuke. I don't want you to have to go through what I had to go through before making my mind up to yield to the spirit and not to my fleshly desires.

Disobedience will rob us from God's anointing. Salvation is free but it cost to be anointed. It cost dying to flesh, it's called suffering for Christ sake. If Jesus had to grow into obedience so do we. And if we want to reign with Him, we must be willing to suffer with Him, suffering for Christ sakes means doing what's right, even when you don't want to.

1Peter 3:13 says, *But and if you suffer for righteousness' sake, happy are you and be not afraid of their terror neither be troubled.* Sometimes we can find ourselves running from our past or old man, afraid what it may do unto us, afraid that we may yield to its desires and be drawn back to darkness.

God created us to be Virtuous Women not a Foolish Woman. If we continue to suffer in this flesh by not obeying it, we will manifest God's idea woman character and integrity. We were born to win, so why allow satan to win this battle that's warring against our mind. Let him know that you are built for suffering because you have the power of God living on the inside of you and you can and will endure every test that comes to try your faith.

If you are struggling with your flesh and turned your back on God. You are not alone, it's not too late to repent and get back in your rightful place.Get back on the Potter's wheel and allow Him to pick up where He left off. He hasn't forsaken or forgotten about you, God is still in that same place you left Him. Waiting for His daughter to come back home.

Most of us need transformation to take place in our lives in order to help us manifest a Virtuous Woman mindset. I can admit to my own failures. I sometimes makes wrong decision spiritual and natural. I too suffer in my flesh, it's not easy doing what's right all the time. We can't live in this flesh without God's Mercy and Grace. Aren't you glad the bible says that the just, shall fall many times, but by the Grace of God, He will pick us back up, so we can finish this race that's set before us?

Let's encourage one another daily to stay on the Potter's wheel and allow our Father to turn our suffering for Christ sakes into a blessing, turn our ashes that comes from our test and tribulation into beauty and turn our pain that comes from suffering for Christ sake into healing.

Chapter 12

Transformation from Past Hurts

As a Pastor's wife, I have compassion for those who holding on to their past hurts and past failures. Those who still choose to live in their old mindset. Not only for women in the body of Christ but those who satan still has full control of as well , those who remain lost in this world without Christ.

I understand how we think as Christians and as a unbelievers. I can relate to those who have a hard time letting go of their past. I also knows how it feels to live in a fleshly mindset that refuses to die. I understand how it feels to be wounded and feeling hopeless.

In this chapter you will recognize how God is with us every step of the way, It doesn't matter what's coming up against our faith to prevent us from becoming a Virtuous Woman. God is willing to turn our ashes into beauty and transform us into the image of a King's daughter, if we patiently endure the race that's set before us.

God Desires Is To Heal Us From Our Past and Give us Hope for the Future by Turning Our Ashes into Beauty: No need to condemn yourself, if you're not walking in the mindsct that pleases God due to past failures. Don't let your past hurts and disappointment cause you to give up hope. God The Potter is still working on us. When He's done you will know it because your transformation will manifest. If you don't believe that God can turn your ashes into beauty it will never happen.

When I'm not walking in the mindset that God has ordained for me to walk in, it grieves the Holy Spirit in me. My heart becomes heavy, causing me to feel unworthy. When we feel unworthy it feeds our old mindset, giving it power over us. We should remind ourselves daily who's in charge of our life, we need to stop trying so hard to be safe and just be save.

To that woman who feeling like giving up and there's no more hope for you. I don't care what struggles or strongholds you are dealing with in your flesh. Know that it's going to be okay. A strong wall may shake but it takes a lot for it to collapse. You stronger than you think you are.

We may fall and slip off the wheel every now and then due to hardship or challenges, but if we immediately hop back on and endure hardship like a King's daughter, we won't yield to that same thing again that caused us to get off the wheel without questioning it first.

Those who God has put back together again, who decide to come back to Him after walking away due to past failures or setbacks can't be destroyed. They too strong to break in pieces and satan knows it. Sometimes life can be very challenge but somebody got to endure it, why not let it be you.

Past failures can cause us to feel hopelessness and God knows that, He is willing to patiently wait on us. He's waiting for us to make up our minds to yield our whole body and soul to Him, so He can begin the process of turning our ashes into beauty. He only see's the best in us and we should see it as well. Keep your head up and don't allow people to tell you that you could never become a virtuous woman by judging your outer appearance.

Tell your fault finders who love to throw stones at you, who has knocked you down a few times, when you up, Thank you. Then give God praise for causing your enemies not only to be your footstool but for helping you build your castle called success. Sometimes those who doubts and look down on us, help push us to the place we should be in Christ.

God will give us joy for our mourning, He will turn our tears that we sometimes shed that comes from us pressing so hard into joy. We must press our way to do whats right in the sight of God. That pressing causes us to press harder towards the mark of the high calling in Christ Jesus. We got the power to go out and be all that God has called us to be, but it's totally up to us to make it happen.

When God sees us pressing towards putting on a Virtuous Woman mindset and turning away from our old foolish mindset, He steps in and turn our mess into a message to help glorify Him and His Kingdom. Lets take a look at what He said in the book of Isaiah.

Isaiah 63:3 says, *"To appoint unto them that mourn in Zion, to give unto them beauty for ashes, the oil of joy for mourning, the garment of praise for the spirit of heaviness; that they might be called trees of righteousness, the planting of the Lord, that he might be glorified.*

God want us to continue pressing and pushing until we birth this (Virtuous) Woman of God. So that He gets the Glory and that other women who in the process of giving up, will have hope not to give up on their vision or dreams. We need to spend our time not focusing on those things that are subject to change, and take off the cares of this world, and place them in the Potter Hands and on Jesus shoulders so that we can walk in total fulfillment.

Jesus healed and freed us from our past and old mindset the day we accepted Him. He's ready to bind up our broken hearts by offering more of His knowledge and wisdom of His word. Our heart and soul sometimes need more of God's word because the wounds from our past are so deep, much too deep for us to heal on our own.

I had some hidden hurts from my past that I had to let go of before receiving God's healing. I can recall rejecting the Hands of God. He wanted to make an exchange with me. He wanted me to give Him my ashes that created hurt and pain in my heart, so He could turn them into beauty. During that season in my life. I felt like I didn't deserve God's best, so I rejected His help for years until I said enough is enough this is not the way I choose to live my life.

A sick heart or soul will reject the wisdom of God. What ever a woman thinks so is she, change the way you think from this day forth. Get your mind right by allowing God to heal you everywhere you hurt. The best decision I made was to turn my life totally to God. Now I can see that woman God's see through His spiritual eyes.

Don't ignore your past hurts instead put them to death by trusting and applying the word of God to your life. Don't just read the word, believe it as well. The word says by Jesus stripes we are healed. Believe It! It says that Jesus took our infirmities, and bare our sicknesses that our heart created. Believe It!!

Jesus is the same Lord yesterday and today. He is able and willing to heal our souls. We don't have to live in a corrupted mindset until we die, our gracious helper the Holy Spirit is willing to guide us every step of the way.

If you continue to read Isaiah 63 you will see that there were many downcast people in Israel. They experienced some past hurts that needed to be turned into joy and I'm sure women was part of that group of people. They had to sell their children into slavery and to become a bondsman. Imagine having your children snatched from you and there is nothing you can do about it?

I'm sure God was touched by their weakness but at the same time didn't use their yoke for excuse, not turned away from their wounded mindset and walk in a wise mindset. A mindset that truly understands how to rely on God when things are going bad. A mindset that will never blame God for their trials and tribulation. We can't allow trouble to turn our heart away from God and our desires to become a better person.

The Bible says we must Glory in our tribulation so that people can see who we trust in. We can't be like Job wife, even though her loss was something that we don't see often in this generation, she chose to walk in a foolish mindset when tribulation hit her home. Instead of relying on God for peace during her great loss, she tried to turn her husband heart away from Him. She didn't turn to God when she was in despair like most of God's children would after losing a child.

Let's have a mindset like Job a man who understood what it meant to be covered with ashes. Job 2:8 says, Then Job scraped his skin with a piece of broken pottery as he sat among the ashes. His wife said to him, "are you still trying to maintain your integrity? Curse God and die.

Though Job was sitting there in pain or ashes, his condition or stay of mind that he was in, could have made a place for the devil to come in and play hop scotch on his mind, after losing everything he had including all of his children. His future look blanked and hopeless, not to forget that satan had placed sickness on his body as well that left him wounded inside and out.

Even his friends turned their back on him, but Job mind was set to wait on his helper the Lord. He was prepared to wait until his change comes from God. He knew who He served and that's a God who lie not. Because Job didn't reject the wisdom and strength from God, he got back double for his suffering.

What are you waiting on God for? What is attacking your faith and mind? What is your greater Test that you go through that's hinder your transformation? Whatever it may be, never give up to the point, that you feel like throwing in the tower. Only those who endure temptation will receive God's best. James (1:2).

I been through some trials and test in my life, that could have made me lost my mind. But by the Grace and Mercy of God. I held on to the hope I had in Christ Jesus. God will never allow anything to come up against His daughters and sons if they can't bare it, He's too faithful to allow such thing to happen.

Just like our children are the world to us, God's children mean the world to Him. He will never allow satan to test us without stepping in, and bring some type of way of escape. God wouldn't tell us not to go back and entangle ourselves in yokes and bondage and allow satan to keep us in bondage. God is not about confusion. He will never tell us to do something He's not willing to do.

I also understand how it feels to struggle with a foolish, corrupt and disturbed mindset and so does our Father. He is aware of what we are going through right now. He understands why we sometimes feel like giving up, in this constant battle that's warring against our flesh. Maybe our tribulation or test aren't as bad as Job's, but even if it is, the same God that delivered his mind and honoured his strength will do the same for us.

If you feel like you been wounded from test and temptation that's warring against your mind, that are assigned by satan to keep you from becoming a wise woman. Know that our Father still turns ashes into beauty. I know that if you desire to become this woman, you have incurred a great loss, I know by experience that satan only tempt those who a threat to him and his kingdom.

I'm a living witness that God will replenish you if you wait on Him. Did He not say, that our later glory shall be greater than our former? If we wait on this great transformation and stay on the Potter's wheel. After we come out the furnace fire, that's testing our faith and identity, we will not be ashamed.

Our minds must be set and ready for battle, we can't give up on what God has started in us. In other words, it would be worth the wait, when we look in the mirror and see that Virtuous Woman of God starring back at us. A woman who been through the fire and understand pain. A woman who refused to bow down to satan easily. A woman who has been shaped and molded for war. Glory to God!

If you are wondering why such a loving God would place us in dark places or throw us in painful situation just to test our faith. Don't put pressure on your brain trying to figure out God. Since the foundation of this world men have being trying to figure Him out. God is a mystery and can't be figure out. God is God and He can do as He please, but He will never tempt us with evil. (James 1:13).

When we decide to follow after ungodly things and go back down that same old path we once traveled releases God's hand of protection to lift and allows satan to tempt us. We can't control suddenly destruction or calamity in this world but when can control how we think by renewing our minds to things of God.

Don't think it strange if you go through so much pain and suffering just to become this wise woman.

You may feel that you don't deserve the test that you going through, maybe you are doing the best you can to live a good life. Whatever landed you in your present predicament, know that God is still in control of your life and will be there for you during every step of the way, if you allow Him by not pushing His hands away.

God's hands are stretched out ready to rescue us from our present pains and sorrow. When we die spiritually from this old mindset and step into a virtuous mindset it will bring honour to us and Glory to God's name. Hold on just a little while longer. Change is coming sooner than you realize, we don't have the time to waist like we did in the past. God will soon send Jesus to rapture up His children from this babylon world and He need us to use the greater in us to help bring others to Christ by sharing our testimonies regarding how He has turned our ashes into beauty.

As I look over my life and see what the Lord has brought me through I give Him all the Glory for turning my ashes into beauty. For turning my mess into something that was not on my to do list a book. When you face your most difficult challenges in life, keep the Faith and know that it will not be like this forever. You coming out in victory, you will not stay in the same mindset you left behind, that mindset before Christ.

Words are Power Use Them To Prophesy Over Your Future and Life:

Prophesy to your own self. Tell your flesh or old man, It may look like you winning in the natural , but in the spiritual realm and by Faith. I'm on the Potter's wheel and He's shaping and molding me into His idea woman, I'm no longer rejecting His help. I'm going to lay still and allow Him to do a perfect work that He has already started in me.

I know that God will never give up on me so why should I give up on Him. Why shouldn't I press towards perfection by dying to my old foolish ways that He has delivered me from through Christ. Why should I continue being disobedient to my Father by choosing not to obey His commandments? Get a vision and see yourself free. Free from all bondages and past hurts.

We claim that we as Christians discern our brothers and sisters spirit to see if it's of God or if it's bad or good. But can't discern satan evil spirit. Do we know satan schemes and deceiving spirit like we claim to know it? Do we see how he works? He convinces us that we can't live on this earth without yielding to our flesh, he whispers lies in our ears today just like he did Eve in the beginning of time.

Changing God's word to make us feel comfortable in our sins are one of satan's schemes. But it ends today, I pray that this book has enlightened your understanding of the battle or war that's going on within our minds. I pray that every stronghold that you are aware of, that's warring against you mind has been exposed and now you are ready to do away with them for good. There's some things that God has brought me out of, that I refuse to go back to, I pray you feel the same way.

I pray after reading this book that women who struggling in their marriage or with being submissive towards their husband and those who has authority over them, mindset will never be the same. I pray that this book has encouraged and Godly rebuked them to the point where they desires change and ready to do what it takes to become a virtuous woman of God.

I pray that you are ready to die to every rebellious spirit that has come against your mindset that has hindered you from obeying God. The next time you find yourself trying to judge another sister or brother by flesh, you will quickly repent and realize, that they could be going through many negative experiences within their mindset just like everybody else.

Now that you have read this book you should know the plan of satan, which is to prevent God's chosen women from walking in the mindset of a virtuous woman. And to keep us in bondage to that old foolish mindset by refusing to change the way we think and from representing Christ in this evil world.

You should know that strongholds, yielding to fleshly desires and walking in a rebellion mindset, holds the key to not receiving the mindset of a Virtuous Woman. God is seeking such women in these last days who are willing to die to our old man or nature and yield more to spiritual things.

God understand the process. We serve a long suffering and faithful Father who is ready to place us on His spiritual wheel as we are then shaped and molded into the image of His Son our Saviour Jesus Christ.

I've made more mistakes, suffered more adversity, overcome more problems, and experienced more failures, just so I can gain the experience that's needed to know how to endure the battle that's set before me. And to also help enlighten the understanding of those who read this book. My flesh took me for a ride but it didn't win the race. Glory to God! You too can overcome that desire or desires that's keeping you from dying to your old foolish woman or mindset.

Writing this book has changed my life tremendously how can anyone write a book with so much truth in it and don't want to follow the guideline or instructions that's in it? Only a few. I no longer look down the sins or shortcomings of others, now I find myself sensitive to their feelings because I understand what it means to struggle in the flesh.

The bible says what the devil meant for our bad, good will turn it around for our good if we love the Lord. At least something good come from my past struggles or weakness, a humble and meek spirit and of course a book title virtuous woman verses foolish woman a constant battle within. I am proof that God will turn our mess into a message, if we chose not to spiritually die during the process. Glory to God!

I know my old man like I know my best friend. I know how to guard my mind and heart because out of it flow the issue of life. I understand the importance of not yielding to my fleshly desires and reject spiritual instruction and feel comfortable in my sins. I going to receive everything God has laid up for me including my spiritual inheritance. I know that only those who willing and obedient shall eat the good of the land. Isaiah 1:19.

If this book has blessed you or changed your life in any way please send your feedback and testimonies to tracym64@gmail.com.

You can also look Co-Pastor Tracy up on her Woman to Woman Let's Talk About It! Group page on Facebook.

God bless you as you take your journey towards becoming God's idea woman.

About the Author

Tracy Mitchell is the Co-Pastor of *Life Changers Worship Center* where she assist her husband Pastor Larry Mitchell in the vision that God has given him. She has 3 children who also have a personal realationship with the Lord.

She is the founder of **Woman to Woman Let's Talk About It Ministry** or Group Page on Facebook that has impacted and encountered so many lives. She has the anointing, realness and boldness to reach the souls of those who ai e lost, and those in the Body of Christ who struggle with their walk with Christ.

If you enjoyed this book or found it useful, I'll be grateful if you would post a short review at **http://www.tracymitchellministries.com**. While you're there you please leave your name and email address to receive updates and latest news and information. Your support really does makes a difference. I read all reviews personally so I can get feedback on how I can make my book better.

www.ingramcontent.com/pod-product-compliance
Lightning Source LLC
Chambersburg PA
CBHW071126090426
42736CB00012B/2025